THE
CHRIST CENTERED COMPANY

37 BIBLICAL BUSINESS HABITS *to*
BUILD *a* THRIVING COMPANY THAT
HONORS GOD *and* BLESSES *the* WORLD

"Darren cuts through the haze so common in the arena of faith and business with these habits, principles, and practical examples of what it looks like to lead in business with Christ at the center of the very enterprise."

—MIKE SHARROW, CEO OF C12 BUSINESS FORUMS

"In Darren Shearer's new book, *The Christ-Centered Company*, a beautiful theological picture emerges about how to manage and operate a business based on biblical principles. Darren has exhaustively researched the Bible and through his insights, case studies, scriptural references, and solid principles he guides the reader through each aspect of business. The real-life case studies and examples throughout the book will assist the reader in finding God's purpose and plan for business. This is a must-read for all believers who own, manage, or supervise any aspect of business."

—BOB HASSON, CEO OF HPCI, CO-HOST OF *EXPLORING THE MARKETPLACE PODCAST*
AUTHOR OF *SHORTCUTS*, *WIRED TO HEAR*, AND *BUSINESS OF HONOR*

"Bravo! *The Christ-Centered Company* is a must-read for any business. As a former Fortune 500 CFO, the values and cultural impact of Jesus on any business detailed in this book are invaluable. Beyond being a helpful guide on how to integrate Jesus and his lessons in business, it is a wonderful resource for our personal lives as well. Darren has created a very practical tool, which will certainly help our companies and ourselves."

—DR. BRUCE HARTMAN, AUTHOR, *JESUS & CO.*
FORMER FORTUNE 500 CHIEF FINANCIAL OFFICER

"*The Christ-Centered Company* is an integral part of our curriculum at Rosedale Bible College and is vital in strengthening the bond between our business school students and the local Christian business community. Our students gain valuable mentorship as they study the book's content with their assigned mentor, and the mentors gain practical guidance on ways to improve their company's culture and operations from a biblical standpoint."

—RICK GRIEST, DIRECTOR OF BUSINESS AND LEADERSHIP,
ROSEDALE BIBLE COLLEGE

"From corporate purpose to philanthropy, from marketing to risk management, Darren skillfully weaves together biblical insights, case studies, and stewardship principles in a first-of-its-kind manual for biblical business management designed for the 21st century. No serious Christ follower eager to do God's will in the marketplace should miss this wonderful work."

—DR. ERNEST LIANG, DIRECTOR, CENTER FOR CHRISTIANITY IN BUSINESS, HOUSTON CHRISTIAN UNIVERSITY

The Christ-Centered Company is a must-read for anyone looking to bring spirituality into the workplace. This book provides a fresh perspective on how to run a business with faith at the center and shows how this approach can lead to greater success and fulfillment. With compelling stories and practical advice, this book is an inspiring and transformative guide for business leaders and entrepreneurs. Whether you are a seasoned executive or just starting out, *The Christ-Centered Company* will help you discover a new way to lead and achieve success in both your personal and professional life."

—LARRY KELLEY, CEO OF CORPORATE CHAPLAINS OF AMERICA

"Darren Shearer did it again with another must-read book for Christ-following business leaders! If you want to be an active part of how God is moving powerfully in the marketplace, *The Christ-Centered Company* is a comprehensive guide that will equip you with practical ways to partner with Him to be a light and a solution in every area of your business."

—SHAE BYNES, AUTHOR, *GRACE OVER GRIND* FOUNDER OF KINGDOM DRIVEN ENTREPRENEUR

"Pragmatically doable. Theologically sound. Activation driven. I challenge you to make *The Christ-Centered Company* your business leadership training manual. And as you do, your business will grow, your impact will multiply, and your legacy will be established."

—DR. JIM HARRIS, AUTHOR, *OUR UNFAIR ADVANTAGE*

"With *The Christ-Centered Company*, Darren Shearer provides an extensive, challenging, and valuable list of 37 biblical business habits that Christian entrepreneurs should aspire to. Well worth reading, re-reading repeatedly, and modelling business practices on."

—MIKE STRATHDEE, EDITOR, *THE MARKETPLACE MAGAZINE*

THE
CHRIST CENTERED COMPANY

37 BIBLICAL BUSINESS HABITS *to* BUILD *a* THRIVING COMPANY THAT HONORS GOD *and* BLESSES *the* WORLD

DARREN SHEARER

HIGH BRIDGE BOOKS
HOUSTON

The Christ-Centered Company
by Darren Shearer

Copyright © 2023 Darren Shearer

Printed in the United States of America
ISBN: 978-1-954943-74-2

High Bridge Books titles may be purchased in bulk for educational, business, fundraising, or sales promotional use. For information, please contact High Bridge Books via www.High-BridgeBooks.com/contact.

Published in Houston, Texas, by High Bridge Books.

Dedicated to my dad, Bob Shearer (1943-2020),
who showed me the kindness, encouragement, and zeal of
our Heavenly Father.

CONTENTS

INTRODUCTION

THE CHRIST-CENTERED COMPANY

*A **Christ-centered company** is a value-making, profit-producing, and law-abiding organization dedicated to spreading the awareness of God's glory through exhibiting Christ-centered, biblical business habits.*

At a pivotal moment in Israel's history, God and God's prophet were put to the test. The question in everyone's mind that day was this: Is the God of Israel more real and powerful than all other gods? Only the one true God would answer by fire and set the altar ablaze.

The prophets of Baal were so convinced of their god's superiority that they "cried out with a loud voice" and began cutting themselves "with swords and lances until blood gushed out on them" to demonstrate their conviction, hoping their god would display his power by igniting their altar (1 Kgs. 18:28).

As during the time of Elijah, a culture war is waging in the world today, and for-profit companies are at the center of it. Considering more than 85 percent of working-age people spend around 65 percent of their waking hours working in a for-profit company, it's clear that the marketplace is the central battleground for competing narratives and ideologies that seek to steer a culture in a particular direction. For-profit companies profoundly influence all levels of society:

- Employees and their families
- Customers
- Suppliers, contractors, & vendors
- Shareholders
- Communities
- Markets → industries → economies → nations

Like the prophets of Baal, the lost world is convinced that their self-obsessed, godless value systems reign supreme in the marketplace, mutilating themselves with values and business practices that suggest our God is dead and irrelevant. Sadly, many professing Christians also conduct business in this way. Sure, marketplace Christians are occasionally told well-meaning platitudes like these:

- "You don't have to leave the business world to do work that glorifies God."
- "God cares about business."
- "The Bible is the best handbook for business."

However, few of us have seen actionable, biblical proof that these things are indeed the case—other than perhaps a proverb here and there.

Of course, the false god Baal never responded. Elijah ridiculed the false prophets, saying,

> Call out with a loud voice, since he is a god; undoubtedly he
> is attending to business, or is on the way, or is on a journey.
> Perhaps he is asleep, and will awaken. (1 Kgs. 18:27)

But then, it was God's and Elijah's turn. Elijah repaired the altar of the Lord that had been torn down by their godless enemies, prepared an offering, drenched it with 12 large jars of water, and asked the Lord to display his glory.

> Then the fire of the Lord fell and consumed the burnt offering
> and the wood, and the stones and the dust; and it licked up
> the water that was in the trench. (1 Kgs. 18:38)

Upon Elijah's order, the prophets of Baal were then executed for high treason, having attempted to highjack the culture God had established for his people through Abraham, Moses, Joshua, and the other patriarchs and matriarchs of our faith.

As was the case in Israel 3,000 years ago, our God is the only one who can answer by fire. He wants you, Marketplace Christian, to devote your company to him as an altar for his glory by centering it on His Son, Jesus Christ. Brightly will it shine in these dark days.

CENTER YOUR COMPANY ON CHRIST.

Yes, a for-profit company cannot be considered as "born-again," for that unspeakable joy and privilege is reserved for individual people who possess a spirit, soul, and body. However, insofar as certain gospel-promoting charities and legal-entity church institutions (i.e., the physical location where you show up on Sunday mornings) can be considered "Christian" organizations—despite that not every person sitting in its rows is truly a born-again follower of Christ—for-profit companies may also be labeled as "Christian" in this regard.

But rather than using "Christian" as an adjective to label a business— or, for that matter, any other organization—perhaps it is more theologically and biblically consistent to label such organizations as "Christ-centered."

My goal with the teachings and process outlined in this book is to help you discover and apply God's will for your business through centering your company on Christ and his Word. As we begin, allow me to offer a working definition of what it means to be a Christ-centered company:

> A *Christ-centered company* is a value-making, profit-producing, and law-abiding organization dedicated to spreading the awareness of God's glory through exhibiting Christ-centered, biblical business habits.

Companies won't remain companies at all if they're not making value, producing profit, and abiding by the laws of the land. (The biblical habits found in this book will help you achieve all three, regardless of your company's core purpose.) The *Christ-centered company* definition's aspect of being "dedicated to spreading the awareness of God's glory" is the key differentiator between a Christ-centered company and those that are centered on something or someone else. This dedication requires that we recognize and seek to reveal the glory of God through every aspect of our companies, "acknowledging Him in all our ways" (Prov. 3:6), which we will seek to do through the Christ-centered company process.

In the definition, what is meant by God's "glory?" The writer of Hebrews said, "The Son is the radiance of God's glory and the exact representation of his being" (Heb. 1:3). There is our answer: Jesus Christ is the glory of God. Thus, we can interpret Habakkuk 2:14 as follows:

> For as the waters fill the sea, the earth [including the business world] will be filled with an awareness of the glory of God [Jesus Christ].

In the verse above, Habakkuk has prophesied the fulfillment of the "Great Commission" Jesus entrusted to his disciples in which he charged his followers to "make disciples of all nations" (Matt. 28:19). The mandate wasn't merely to "go and make profit," "go and plant churches," or "go and make a difference"—although these are strategically significant in our primary mission as God's people. Instead, it's to "go and make *disciples*." Collectively, individual disciples of Jesus are called to disciple entire groups of people—that is, to reveal Jesus (i.e., "the glory of God") throughout all spheres of all cultures in all societies.

COMPANIES MARKET CULTURE.
CULTURE MAKES DISCIPLES.
INFLUENCERS' HABITS MAKE CULTURE.

Your company's culture is the primary thing your company is marketing. The products, services, operations, values, and policies of your company flow from your company's culture. Team members come and go, but the culture of your company will remain. Your company's culture will be influenced and defined by every team member's habits for as long as the company endures. If you want to carry out the Great Commission by "making disciples" in the world, center your company's culture and habits on Christ.

Culture can be defined as "the defining habits of a group of people." People's habits shape the culture of your company, and if those habits are

Christ-centered, the culture will make disciples of Jesus Christ. As this corporate disciple-making happens in a company, the company becomes increasingly Christ-centered. In a Christ-centered company, Jesus is revealed through the leaders of the company and, ultimately, throughout its entire culture and prevailing habits. When aligned with this disciple-making mission in word and deed, Christ-centered companies can be used as tools to help individuals, communities, nations, and industries recognize the glorious image and character of Jesus.

This process usually begins when one person of influence in a company decides to partner with God in his disciple-making mission. Will you be that person on behalf of your company?

WHAT GETS MEASURED GETS DONE.

Either before, during, or after you read this book, please take the *Christ-Centered Company Assessment* online at TheologyofBusiness.com/CCC to assess the extent to which your company's culture and habits are currently consistent with the Christ-centered company habits taught in this book. This book provides real-world best practices and practical biblical commentary for all 37 habits surveyed in the assessment. Each is categorized into one of the following seven parts:

1. Corporate Purpose and Culture

2. Marketing, Sales, and Customer Care

3. Accounting and Accountability

4. People Management

5. Business Law and Conflict

6. Risk Management

7. Philanthropy

You will be asked to rate your company—and, in a few cases, yourself, as an influencer within the company—on a scale of one to five. If you give yourself or your company a score of five, this means you and/or your company *always* demonstrate adherence to that particular habit while a score of one means you and/or your company *never* demonstrate adherence to that particular habit.

How different would your company be—for you, your team members, your customers, and every other stakeholder who encounters your company—if you could honestly give yourself and your company a five-out-of-five rating in all 37 habit statements in the *Christ-Centered Company Assessment*? Does this sound unrealistically utopian? Impossible? Excessive? More on these objections in a moment.

Having studied Christ-centered companies and God's Word concerning business for more than a decade, interviewed hundreds of Christian business leaders and academics active in faith-and-business integration, and implemented these habits to varying degrees as a full-time small business owner and CEO myself since 2013, I have observed that these 37 habits are the most consistently applied best practices among companies whose influencers deliberately aim to use their companies as platforms for revealing God's glory to impact culture.

Rather than giving examples in the book from today's companies for whom Christ is unwelcome and decidedly irrelevant, the real-world examples in this book have been deliberately restricted to companies whose leaders have publicly indicated that their companies exist for God's purposes.

Whereas I focused on marketplace Christians' individual marketplace callings and assignments in my previous book, *The Marketplace Christian*, this book focuses on God's will and ways for a for-profit company *corporately*.

The approach I have taken in developing this book is similar to the one I took with writing *Marketing Like Jesus*, except this book focuses on more aspects of business than just marketing, and the scope of biblical application encompasses the whole Bible rather than being limited to the earthly life and ministry of Jesus as recorded in the four Gospels—Matthew, Mark, Luke, and John.

Before we begin this book, allow me to address some of the objections that could hold some Christian business influencers back from fully committing to the process of partnering with the Holy Spirit to transform one's own company into one that is Christ-centered.

OBJECTION 1 - "MOST OF OUR TEAM MEMBERS AND CUSTOMERS AREN'T CHRISTIANS."

Yes, in today's post-Christian society, it's likely that most of your team members and customers aren't followers of Jesus Christ and consider God as fictitious, irrelevant, and/or counterproductive to their lives.

And there have been enough infamous discrimination lawsuits filed against Christian-influenced companies to strike fear in the hearts of anyone seeking to use a for-profit company as a platform for bringing glory to God in any observable way.

Fortunately, you can work toward implementing all 37 of the Christ-centered company habits across your company without publicly announcing to the entire company that your objective is to partner with God to transform the whole outfit into a Christ-centered company. You don't have to put a Christian fish or cross on your company's logo. Verbally announcing such a commitment from the outset won't reveal God's glory nearly to the extent that stealthily and shrewdly implementing the 37 Christ-centered company habits will. There is tremendous power in applying God's Word in the process of stewarding what God has entrusted. You don't have to broadcast your intentions to everyone in the company to cultivate a Christ-centered company. In most cases, it's better if you don't take that approach.

In fact, if you were to present the complete list of 37 Christ-centered company habits to each of your team members without telling them the source of those habits, it's highly unlikely they would object to more than perhaps a few of them (i.e., the few that mention "God," "Jesus," or "Bible" explicitly). As you implement all these habits, most of your people will thank you, regardless of their demographics. You can bank on that.

Christianity might even be illegal in the place where your company operates. Again, you don't have to broadcast your Christ-centered motives to everyone (e.g., the government, your employees, etc.). Just apply the habits and watch God display his glory however he desires.

OBJECTION 2 - "MY BUSINESS PARTNER ISN'T A CHRISTIAN."

If your business partner is truly against your commitment to apply the 37 Christ-centered company habits, it's likely that you are "unequally yoked with an unbeliever" (2 Cor. 6:14). It might be time to part ways.

But if your business partner isn't actively against you and your efforts to apply these habits, why not assume he is for you? As Jesus said, "Whoever is not against us is for us" (Mark 9:40). Don't allow your business partner's lack of devotion to God to sabotage the work he wants to do in and through your company.

Who knows? This could be your greatest opportunity to show your business partner that God knows and cares more about your company than he does.

OBJECTION 3 - "I'M NEITHER THE OWNER NOR THE CO-OWNER OF THE COMPANY."

To be sure, it's easier to apply these habits in your company if you're the company's sole owner; or, at least, there are fewer excuses for not applying them.

Even if you're not the owner or co-owner, that doesn't mean you don't share responsibility for applying many of the Christ-centered company habits to some degree. You have some level of influence in your company or else they wouldn't be paying you. For this reason, I will generally refer to the reader of this book as a "Christ-centered company influencer," lest it be assumed I'm only speaking to the senior leaders of your company. Regardless of your job title, consider accepting at least partial responsibility for everything that happens in your company. Even if you're the lowest-ranking entry-level employee, you still have God-given authority and influence to pray for your company, advocate for necessary changes, and demonstrate the changes you desire to see across your company. As you do so, you will likely find yourself getting promoted within your company.

If you aren't in senior leadership within your company but know of a senior leader who desires to see God's glory revealed at your place of work, consider giving a copy of this book to her and see if she would be interested in committing to the Christ-centered company process with you. Imagine

-- 8 --

how God might use such a step of faith to impact your company and its stakeholders!

OBJECTION 4 - "MY COMPANY IS TOO SMALL TO DO ALL THESE THINGS."

Many of the company leaders who have already taken the *Christ-Centered Company Assessment* have proven that every Bible-based business habit you're going to read about in this book can indeed be applied in a for-profit company.

With that said, this will be a long-term process for you and your company, with frequent recalibration required to stay on track.

I suggest that, if you are committed to the process of growing yourself and your company in all 37 habits and have surrendered ultimate control of your company to the Holy Spirit—relying on Him as your source of power and wisdom to apply these habits from God's Word—your company is operating as a Christ-centered company.

GROWING YOUR COMPANY TO MATURITY

One generally accepted definition of a *mature company* is "one that is well-established in its industry with a well-known product and loyal customer following." Aside from the number of employees it has or the level of its gross revenue or profitability, I suggest that a *mature* Christ-centered company is one that averages at least a 90 percent rating in all seven parts of the 37 Christ-centered company habit statements.

When you stand before God one day, he's likely not going to ask you, "How many employees did you have?" or "What was your gross (or net) revenue?" However, among many other things, he will likely ask something more like this: "By the standard of my Word, how mature was the company I entrusted to you?"

HOW TO READ THIS BOOK

Every Christian business influencer (e.g., business owner, leader, senior manager, middle manager, etc.) should take the *Christ-Centered Company*

Assessment, discuss the results with their teams and peers, learn the biblical business operating system presented in this book, and commit to forming biblical business habits throughout the companies they influence.

To get the most out of this book, I suggest reading it with your leadership team and/or a peer advisory group of other Christian business influencers. Ask each person in the study group to take the online assessment on their own and then be ready to report their results to the group as your group's study moves from one habit to the next. Discussion questions have been provided at the end of each habit's commentary to help you facilitate your group's conversation.

As other members of your company's leadership team take the assessment, find out if different people gave different responses. Identify and discuss what your company is doing well and which areas need to be improved.

If you're studying the book with a group of peers from other companies, identify best practices from the group members' companies that you may find helpful and appropriate to implement in your own company.

As you identify areas needing improvement, delegate the responsibility for those improvements to your team members who are accountable for those areas. Of course, bear in mind that the leader is ultimately responsible for your company's past and future performance regarding each habit.

Most of all, invite the Holy Spirit—your helper and guide into all truth (John 16:13)—to give you the wisdom and power to grow in each of these 37 habits.

Now, let's begin!

REFLECTION, DISCUSSION, AND APPLICATION

How do for-profit companies fit into God's mission to redeem humanity?

Are any of the "four objections" holding you back from cultivating a Christ-centered company at your place of work?

From a biblical standpoint, which areas of your company are mature? Which are immature?

PART 1

CORPORATE PURPOSE AND CULTURE

Follow this QR code to take the
Christ-Centered Company Assessment.

HABIT 1

RECOGNIZE JESUS IS ON THE RECEIVING END

As a leader of my company, I choose to work for Jesus Christ and recognize He is on the receiving end of every action taken in my company.

Whatever you do, work at it with all your heart, as working for the Lord, not for human masters, since you know that you will receive an inheritance from the Lord as a reward. It is the Lord Christ you are serving.

—Colossians 3:23-24, NIV

Truly I say to you, to the extent that you did it for one of the least of these brothers or sisters of Mine, you did it for Me ... to the extent that you did not do it for one of the least of these, you did not do it for Me, either.

—Matthew 25:40, 45b

The fear of the Lord is the beginning of wisdom, And the knowledge of the Holy One is understanding.

—Proverbs 9:10

Who do you work *for* in business? Who do the people in your company work *for*?

I ask my company's managers never to think or say, "I work *for* High Bridge Books & Media." And Heaven forbid they ever think or say, "I work for Darren Shearer." Instead, I encourage them to cultivate this perspective: "I work *with* High Bridge Books & Media; I work *for* Jesus." (Even if your employees aren't Christians, it's still better to encourage them to say they work "with" rather than "for" you and your company.)

This is *the* foundational habit for cultivating a Christ-centered company: "Whatever you do, work at it with all your heart, as working for the Lord, not for human masters" (Col. 3:23, NIV). A company can only be considered *Christ-centered* to the extent that its influencers decide to work for Jesus and not for anyone or anything else. In all its operations, a Christ-centered company's culture promotes the perspective and attitude that Jesus is on the receiving end of everything done in and through the business, which ought to compel us to seek and apply his will for the company.

JESUS IS THE CEO, CHAIRMAN, AND OWNER ... BUT SO MUCH MORE.

Perhaps you're familiar with the common temptation to act one way around the company's senior leaders while acting differently around the company's less-influential stakeholders. I think this phenomenon is why I have found it somewhat easier to view Jesus as the head of the company I manage (e.g., CEO, owner, chairman-of-the-board, etc.) than to view him in all the other roles related to the company. This Deistic view of God—the idea that God is so high-and-lifted-up that he's disengaged from the seemingly trivial aspects of a company—explains how we can assume we're interacting with people one way while simultaneously interacting with God another.

Unlike a human boss, Jesus is omnipresent through his Holy Spirit, interacting with us through every relationship and operation in the company. He is on the receiving end of everything done in and through the company, "For from Him, and through Him, and to Him are all things" (Rom. 11:36a). An employee at lawnmower-maker Walker Manufacturing reflected this truth when he said,

I treat every lawnmower that I'm making like Christ is going to be getting that lawnmower. So I want to make sure everything is just perfect on it.[1]

Some Christ-centered companies keep an empty seat at their boardroom table to help them remember that Jesus is the chairman of the board. What would happen if, in addition to viewing Jesus in the most influential roles of the companies we manage, we also operated as though Jesus fills every other position in relation to our companies?

- Entry-level team member
- Team member's family member
- Customer/client
- Prospective customer/client
- Supervisor
- Intern
- Supplier/contractor
- Vendor
- Minority shareholder
- Consultant
- Person on the other side of a lawsuit
- Board member
- Chairman of the board
- Competitor
- IRS agent
- Accountant
- City official
- Owner
- Yourself
- Anyone else you interact with in business

The ways in which we and the companies we manage relate to each of these people is exactly how we and our teams are treating Jesus. This awareness of God's omnipresence helps us to believe that he is truly omniscient (i.e., all-knowing) concerning everything that affects us and our companies.

What would happen to our business habits if we truly viewed God as being on the receiving end of *everything* we do in business? Not just the "big picture" stuff. Not just the hard decisions. Not just the personal morality issues. Not just the charitable giving. Everything.

What would happen to your customer service if you viewed your customers as Jesus?

How much stronger would your product quality be if you viewed each end user as Jesus?

What would happen to your employee compensation and employee care programs if you viewed your team members and their families as Jesus?

How much more thorough and ethical would your accounting habits be if you viewed that IRS agent who reviews your company's tax return as Jesus?

What would happen to your advertising habits if you viewed that impressionable viewer or listener as Jesus?

Jesus assures us,

> Truly I say to you, to the extent that you did it for one of the
> least of these brothers or sisters of Mine, you did it for Me ...
> to the extent that you did not do it for one of the least of these,
> you did not do it for Me, either. (Matt. 25:40, 45b)

In different ways, everyone with whom we interact in business is one of the "least of these." This is not to minimize the plight of the materially poor among us. Poverty takes many forms as Jesus also tells us that those who think they are rich are actually "wretched, miserable, poor, blind, and naked" (Rev. 3:17b). The point is how we treat people in business is exactly how we're treating Jesus. He is on the receiving end of every thought, word, deed, and output that flows from the companies we manage. As C.S. Lewis said in *The Four Loves*, "See the face of Christ in every man and act accordingly."

This mindset helps cultivate "the fear of the Lord [which] is the beginning of wisdom" (Prov. 9:10). It's impossible to operate with wisdom in the marketplace without realizing that everything we think, say, and do is ultimately thought, said, and done toward Jesus. Not only should this put the fear of the Lord in us, but it should also help us realize we have far more opportunities to honor Jesus in business than perhaps we originally thought.

As we remain aware that Jesus is on the receiving end, we'll seek him more fervently for guidance on how to worship and honor him through our business relationships and practices. We'll grow in our awareness that he is working through each person with whom we work to conform us and our companies to his will. The opportunity we have to transform our companies through revealing Jesus is part of God's "final restoration of *all things* as God promised long ago through his holy prophets" (Acts 3:21, emphasis mine). The marketplace—and your company in particular—are key aspects of "all things" God aims to restore.

You work *for* Jesus. You work *with* people. Your company is simply the context for you and your colleagues in the marketplace to become more like Jesus, causing the awareness of his glory to be revealed throughout the earth "as the waters cover the sea" (Hab. 2:14).

On this foundational habit and mindset, we can build Christ-centered companies.

REFLECTION, DISCUSSION, AND APPLICATION

Is it hard to view Jesus on the receiving end of everything done in and through your company? Why or why not?

Where do you consistently view Jesus Christ as being on the receiving end of what happens in and through your company?

In which aspect of your company is it hardest to see Jesus on the receiving end?

---

1 "Making Beautiful Places for the Glory of God," Center for Faith and Work, LeTourneau University, October 1, 2013, educational video, Vimeo.com/75906040.

HABIT 2

RELY ON GOD'S PRESENCE, POWER, AND WISDOM

As a leader of my company, I invite God's presence, power, and wisdom into my company through praying continually, worshiping the Lord, and meditating on God's Word.

The Lord replied, "My Presence will go with you, and I will give you rest." Then Moses said to him, "If your Presence does not go with us, do not send us up from here."

—Exodus 33:14-15

I am the vine, you are the branches; the one who remains in Me, and I in him bears much fruit, for apart from Me you can do nothing.

—John 15:5

Unless the Lord builds the house, They labor in vain who build it; Unless the Lord guards the city, The watchman keeps awake in vain.

—Psalm 127:1

Pray continually.

—2 Thessalonians 5:17

But Jesus Himself would often slip away to the wilderness and pray.

—Luke 5:16

S imon Peter and his crew had been fishing all night but caught nothing. Then, Jesus showed up and told them what to do to succeed in their work. Even though his instructions defied their experience-based logic, they listened, obeyed, and caught so many fish that they had to call for more boats to haul it in.

> He said to Simon, "Put out into the deep water and let down your nets for a catch." Simon responded and said, "Master, we worked hard all night and caught nothing, but I will do as You say and let down the nets." And when they had done this, they caught a great quantity of fish, and their nets began to tear; so they signaled to their partners in the other boat to come and help them. And they came and filled both of the boats, to the point that they were sinking. (Luke 5:1-7)

As with Simon Peter, Jesus cares about your business. More than that, he desires close friendship and constant communication with you. Invite him in. He's already there.

GOD IS MORE THAN HABITS, STRATEGIES, AND TACTICS.

In this book, we're exploring 37 priceless, biblical habits for business. But it's possible to exploit many of God's principles without a relationship with God himself. Christians and non-Christians alike can apply the Bible's timeless business wisdom and experience the benefits while never truly

— 20 —

knowing God who established those principles. With only a set of timeless truths, we are left with nothing but rules and best practices yet no friendship with the Lord. Like Moses, God offers us so much more. Not only does God want you to work *for* him (i.e., Habit 1), he wants you to work *with* him.

God promised Moses, "My presence shall go with you, and I will give you rest" (Exod. 33:14). Like Moses, most of us would agree that we want God's presence in our lives and organizations. But we get distracted. Then, we move ahead without him, forfeiting the friendship he desires to have with us.

But this was not the case with Moses. Moses said, "If Your presence does not go with us, do not lead us up from here" (Exod. 33:15). Even if it meant missing out on the Promised Land, the fulfillment of his God-given vision, Moses refused to go anywhere without the presence, power, and wisdom of God.

The Bible says of Moses, "So the Lord used to speak to Moses face to face, just as a man speaks to his friend" (Exod. 33:11a). Let's pursue that level of relationship with God and refuse to settle for a relationship with mere doctrine, do's, and don'ts. Don't settle for a relationship with good biblical best practices, strategies, and tactics for your business. Go after an intimate relationship with God through the person of the Holy Spirit he provided for us. Being a Christ-centered company isn't just about centering your company on the teachings of Jesus and the Bible. It's about centering yourself and your company on the actual person of Jesus through his Holy Spirit, the "Spirit of Christ" (Rom. 8:9). The Holy Spirit is the only God on the planet today.

WISDOM IS A PERSON.

As you seek to discover and apply God's will for your business, recognize that wisdom is God himself, not merely a set of how-to's. The Bible says, "It is due to Him that you are in Christ Jesus, who *became to us wisdom from God*" (1 Cor. 1:30). Welcome God into your life and business through the person of the Holy Spirit, and you will have his friendship and wisdom to refine your motives, guide your decisions, and breathe life into your efforts.

Practically speaking, how can we welcome the Holy Spirit into our companies and cultivate friendship with him?

PRAY AND WORSHIP GOD CONTINUALLY.

The Bible says, "Pray continually" (2 Thess. 5:17). How often is "continually?" I take that to mean God wants to be in constant conversation with us, more than just the times when we bow our heads and close our eyes (e.g., at mealtimes, when confronted with a crisis, etc.). It has been said, "Prayer is our spiritual breathing." When do we not need to breathe? When do we not need an intimate awareness of God's presence, character, and will in our lives throughout the day?

Many of us have asked, "How am I supposed to be praying while I'm working?" Praying continually doesn't mean we're speaking to God all the time. It's especially about cultivating a constant awareness of him. As 17th-century Carmelite friar Brother Lawrence said in the book of his collected teachings, *Practicing the Presence of God*,

> There is not in the world a kind of life more sweet and delightful, than that of a continual conversation with God; those only can comprehend it who habit and experience it.

Norm Miller, founder of Interstate Batteries, offers his explanation of what it means to "pray continually."

> I finally discovered that it's an attitude of prayer you can have on an ongoing basis during your waking hours, regardless of what you are doing or where you are. It's an inner dialogue with God, a communion of dependence and trust in thought with Him.[1]

Like me, you probably get distracted from continual prayer. The Bible tells us, "Devote yourselves to prayer, *keeping alert in it with an attitude of thanksgiving*" (Col. 4:2, emphasis mine). Begin thinking of everything with which God has blessed you. Allow that attitude of thanksgiving to overflow from your heart throughout the day, keeping your mind fixated on God, his goodness, and his desires. That's one way to "pray continually."

PRAY AND WORSHIP GOD AT SET TIMES.

Starting a few years ago, upon the suggestion of a fellow Christian CEO, I set three alarms on my phone: 10am, 2pm, and 6pm. When the alarms go off (usually just a quiet buzz), I pause for a few moments—often while opening my hands—quietly release my current worries to God, and express my gratitude for his goodness. Regardless of how busy and distracted I get, those alarms will go off no matter what, reminding me to keep my heart and mind focused on the Lord and his presence.

Although it's a good first step toward getting into a lifestyle of praying continually, a few brief moments throughout the day aren't long enough to cultivate the level of spiritual awareness we need to sustain us for an entire day. As such, there's no substitute for setting aside more extended times to sit before the Lord in prayer, Bible study, and worship.

The most obvious benefit of praying at set times for at least 10 minutes is the extended time to restore your focus on the Lord. Early morning is an ideal opportunity to spend devotional time with the Lord because that experience will form your first impression of the day, setting the tone to keep you in tune with him as the day progresses. The Bible says, "But Jesus Himself would often slip away to the wilderness and pray" (Luke 5:16). Let's follow Christ's example and spend time alone with our Heavenly Father regularly.

READ THE BIBLE REGULARLY.

Reading the Bible daily properly frames, colors, and informs the ongoing conversations we ought to be having with God concerning our companies and everything else in our lives. Without a proper understanding of God and his will as expressed in the Bible, how can we be sure the prayer conversations we're having are with God and not just with our own sinful nature or with Satan in disguise, which seek to sabotage our relationship with God and others?

Every day (well, I have missed a few), I read through a chapter of the Bible and send one verse that stood out to me to another brother-in-Christ via text message. In that daily text message, I also include one thought or prayer I had in response to that verse (or set of verses)—although that part isn't required. As I write this, today's reading is the fourth chapter of 1 John.

In turn, my brother-in-Christ does the same. We call it Bible Texting Accountability (BTA), an incredibly simple and powerful method for staying consistent with daily Bible reading.

Find a method that works for you and stay in God's Word daily.

PRAY TOGETHER WITH AND FOR YOUR TEAM.

If you have the authority to pray at your company's meetings, don't be afraid to do it. According to Alliance Defending Freedom, "Employers can [legally] hold regular devotionals like prayer meetings or chapel services for employees, so long as attendance is voluntary."[2]

If you know one of your team members is struggling with something in her personal life, offer to pray for her right there in your workplace (or over Zoom if you're working virtually). At High Bridge Books & Media, we pray for our team members and clients at the end of each staff meeting.

Even if the employees at your company aren't Christians, you'll likely find they would welcome the opportunity to have a caring co-worker pray with them concerning struggles they are facing.

Prayer is your most useful tool for welcoming God's presence, power, and guidance into your company. It is your most powerful tool for cultivating a Christ-centered culture in your company. Ask the Holy Spirit to help you pray continually, pray at set times daily, read and meditate on God's Word daily, and pray together with your team.

REFLECTION, DISCUSSION, AND APPLICATION

On a personal level, what does "praying continually" look like in your everyday life?

Do you pray and worship at set times and/or for extended times? How?

Do you read the Bible daily? What is your strategy for staying consistent?

Do you pray with and for your team members? When? How often?

1 Norm Miller, *Beyond the Norm* (Nashville: Thomas Nelson, 1996), 154.

2 Alliance Defending Freedom, *Faith in the Workplace: Legal Protections for Christians Who Own or Lead a Business* (2023), 3.

Habit 3

Establish a Christ-Centered Purpose Statement

Our company has a clear and Christ-centered statement of purpose that explains why we exist as a company and is well-understood by our company's team members.

Where there is no vision, the people are unrestrained ...

—Proverbs 29:18a

Then the Lord answered me and said, "Write down the vision and inscribe it clearly on tablets, so that one who reads it may run."

—Habakkuk 2:2

Twice in the book of Judges, we are told, "In those days there was no king in Israel; everyone did what was right in his own eyes" (Judg. 17:6; 21:25). One reason for the moral chaos that ravaged Israel during the time of the judges was the lack of a singular purpose that would have otherwise been provided by a righteous king with a righteous vision.

Likewise, your team members and other stakeholders will be indifferent (or even resistant) toward your company unless they have a clear sense of why your company exists and where you are leading the organization. Without this consistent clarity, Proverbs says your team members will be "unrestrained," which will make it extremely difficult for them to support the work God has called you to do in the marketplace. Without a compelling sense of purpose to bridle their attention and energy, such people are only looking for a mere transaction (e.g., paycheck, purchase, etc.), and they'll leave your company as soon as a slightly better deal comes along.

A statement of core purpose is more than a definition of *what* you do or *how* you do it. It's a statement of *why* you do it. Simon Sinek said it well: "People don't buy *what* you do; they buy *why* you do it." As Christ-centered company influencers, it's our responsibility to make this purpose consistently clear for our team members and other stakeholders.

Habakkuk 2:2 says, "Then the Lord answered me and said, 'Write down the vision and inscribe it clearly on tablets, so that one who reads it may run.'" Like Habakkuk, if we present our *why* with consistent clarity, our team members and other stakeholders can start running alongside in our shared direction and stay on course.

WHAT DOES IT MEAN FOR A STATEMENT OF CORE PURPOSE TO BE "CHRIST-CENTERED?"

Some Christ-centered companies have elected to mention God explicitly in their statements of core purpose. Here are eight examples:

- Gulf Winds International – "To glorify God by providing world-class logistics services through continual investment in our people, clients, community, and the world we live in."[1]

- Turbocam – "To honor God, create wealth for its employees and support Christian service to God and people."[2]

- 4 Rivers Smokehouse – "We exist to use our God-given gifts to support the local community through exceptional products, steadfast customer service, and uncompromised integrity."[3]

- Texas Injection Molding – "We exist to use our gifts and talents to be the best supplier to our customers, the best employer to our team, the best customer to our suppliers, and to declare thanksgiving to our Lord for His provision."[4]

- Chick-fil-A – "To glorify God by being a faithful steward of all that is entrusted to us. To have a positive influence on all who come in contact with Chick-fil-A."[5]

- Interstate Batteries – "To glorify God and enrich lives as we deliver the most trustworthy source of power to the world."[6]

- Correct Craft – "To build boats for the glory of God."[7]

- SonicAire – "To show God's goodness to our partners and communities through proven fugitive dust solutions that create safer, healthier and more efficient work environments."[8]

While the founders of these Christ-centered companies explicitly mention God in their statements of core purpose, this isn't a requirement to be considered a Christ-centered company. There isn't a single mention of God in the entire book of Esther, yet the entire book is about God. Because your statement of core purpose must be shared by all your company's team members, regardless of their religious affiliations, it's sometimes better to use Estherian, religiously neutral language in your company's statement of core purpose.

What's most important is that you and the other Christ-followers who influence your company understand the biblical, Christ-centered basis for whatever your statement of core purpose happens to be. You all should be able to answer this question: "How does fulfilling our core purpose reveal the will and ways of God?" To help you think through this, Tim Keller says there is "biblical warrant" for each of these motivations for work although they are each prioritized differently among marketplace Christians:

- To further social justice in the world
- To be personally honest and evangelize your colleagues
- To do skillful, excellent work
- To create beauty

- To work from a Christian motivation to glorify God, seeking to engage and influence culture to that end
- To work with a grateful, joyful, gospel-changed heart through all the ups and downs
- To do whatever gives you the greatest joy and passion
- To make as much money as you can, so that you can be as generous as you can[9]

Even if you choose to write your company's purpose statement in religiously neutral language, how will accomplishing that purpose bring glory to God?

MAKE IT PLAIN.

It's not enough to go through the exercise of defining your company's *why*; it must be easily explained and understood by all your company's team members, customers, and other stakeholders. Only then can it permeate the entire culture and operations of your company.

When I speak with authors interested in publishing their books through our company, High Bridge Books, I always make sure the author understands *why* we do what we do. I have found this is a much more effective way to recruit the right authors than simply telling them about the specific features of the publishing services we offer. Here's what I tell them:

We help Christ-centered authors build a legacy by crafting and publishing messages and stories that reflect God's glory in all spheres of culture.[10]

We don't just publish books. We help authors build their legacies and reflect God's glory through the messages and stories they share with the world.

REFLECTION, DISCUSSION, AND APPLICATION

In 1-2 statements or sentences that will be easily understood by all who interact with your company, why does your company exist? Write it down and share it with everyone.

How does your "why" statement reveal the will and ways of God?

---

[1] https://www.gwii.com/about/.

[2] https://www.turbocam.com/about.

[3] https://www.4rsmokehouse.com/about/.

[4] https://texasinjectionmolding.com/about/vision-and-core-values/.

[5] https://www.chick-fil-a.com/careers/culture.

[6] https://www.interstatebatteries.com/about/our-culture.

[7] https://www.ncfgiving.com/stories/building-boats-for-the-glory-of-god.

[8] https://www.sonicaire.com/about-sonicaire-combustible-dust-control/.

[9] Tim Keller, *Every Good Endeavor* (New York: Penguin, 2012), 22.

[10] https://www.highbridgebooks.com.

Habit 4

Define and Promote Your Core Values

Our company has a clear and Christ-centered set of core values to express our core purpose that is well-understood by our company's team members.

These words, which I am commanding you today, shall be on your heart. And you shall repeat them diligently to your sons and speak of them when you sit in your house, when you walk on the road, when you lie down, and when you get up. You shall also tie them as a sign to your hand, and they shall be as frontlets on your forehead. You shall also write them on the doorposts of your house and on your gates.

—Deuteronomy 6:6-9

Finally, brothers and sisters, whatever is true, whatever is honorable, whatever is right, whatever is pure, whatever is lovely, whatever is commendable, if there is any excellence and if anything worthy of praise, think about these things.

—Philippians 4:8

The children of Israel were taught to think and talk about God's commandments constantly. This would help them keep God's values at the forefront of their minds throughout the day, influencing their thoughts and actions at home, work, and everywhere else. There was not a single context in which they were not expected to meditate on God's character, values, will, and ways.

Likewise, your company's Christ-centered core values should form the basis for how your company will express its core purpose to your team members, customers, and other stakeholders. These values should be top-of-mind for all your team members as they make decisions on behalf of your company.

YOUR COMPANY ALREADY HAS CORE VALUES.

Whether you realize it or not, your company's culture has already established a hierarchy of prevailing values that magnify and solidify the culture that currently defines your company.

The problem is, of course, the values that have organically infiltrated and dominated your company may be counterproductive to what you believe is the company's Christ-centered identity and purpose. Examples of such counterproductive values may include the following:

- Win at any cost.
- Never admit when you're wrong.
- Do just enough to get by.
- Always appear to share the same values as the broader culture.
- Destroy the competition.
- Prove that you're the smartest person in the room.
- It's okay as long as you don't get caught.

Without being deliberate and aggressive about identifying and teaching core values that will help your company grow its Christ-centered culture, it's inevitable that counterproductive values like the ones mentioned above will dominate and shape the destiny of your company.

If you've lost control of the value system in your company, the good news is you can still be the godly influence needed to shift the culture back in the right direction.

WHAT SHOULD YOUR CORE VALUES BE?

Paul provides a handy checklist to guide us in the process of establishing core values for our organizations. He says these are the kinds of things we (and our team members) should be thinking about all the time:

- Whatever is true
- Whatever is honorable
- Whatever is right
- Whatever is pure
- Whatever is lovely
- Whatever is commendable
- Any excellence
- Anything worthy of praise

Establishing core values for your organization doesn't need to be complicated and time-consuming. Aside from making sure your core values are consistent with the items in Paul's Philippians 4:8 list, there are only a few criteria that are essential to establishing core values for your company:

1. Ask God in prayer to show you the right core values.
2. Ensure your core values are expressions of your company's actual core purpose and identity.
3. Invite feedback from your team members.
4. Limit the number of core values to no more than 3-4. (Otherwise, it may be difficult for you and your team to give each one the focus needed to get your team rowing in the same direction.)

As with your statement of core purpose, you don't need to explicitly mention God for your core values to be Christ-centered.

When I served in the U.S. Air Force, I was constantly reminded that the USAF's three core values are 1) integrity, 2) service before self, and 3) excellence in all we do. These three concepts might seem generic to some, but for a follower of Jesus Christ, they are absolutely Christ-centered, consistent with Philippians 4:8, and effective for cultivating the kind of outstanding corporate culture I proudly experienced as an officer in the U.S. Air Force from 2004 to 2008. Who has been more integrous, service-oriented, and excellent than Jesus? These are examples of Christ-centered values we should all hold dear.

PROMOTE YOUR CORE VALUES IN STRATEGIC PLACES AND AT STRATEGIC TIMES THROUGHOUT YOUR COMPANY.

Horst Schulze, former CEO of the Ritz-Carlton Hotel Company and current CEO of Capella Hotels and Resorts, was the leader of the first hospitality company to win the coveted Malcolm Baldridge National Quality Award. Horst has revolutionized the hospitality industry through exceptional service, consistency, and his commitment to Christ. (Fun fact: After hearing workers consistently say "my pleasure" during a stay at a Ritz-Carlton hotel that was under Horst Schultze's leadership, Truett Cathy liked it so much that he began requiring all Chick-fil-A workers to start saying the signature line when thanked by a customer.)

At Capella Hotels and Resorts, Horst established 24 standards for how the Capella Hotels and Resorts team members would be expected to treat customers and fellow team members, expressions of the company's vision "to be the global leader in the service business." Here are some examples from this list, which Horst titled the "Capella Canon."

> #4 – We assist each other, stepping out of our primary duties to effectively provide service to our guests.

> #5 – You are responsible to identify and immediately correct defects before they affect a guest. Defect prevention is key to service excellence.

#7 – Ensure all areas of the hotel are immaculate. We are responsible for cleanliness, maintenance, and organization.

#8 – Always recognize guests. Interrupt whatever activity you are doing when a guest is within 3 meters (12 feet), greet them with a smile and offer assistance.

#11 – When a guest encounters any difficulty, you are responsible to own it and start the problem resolution process. You are empowered to resolve any problem to the guest's complete satisfaction.

#12 – Escort guests until they are comfortable with the directions or make visual contact with their destination. Do not point.

#17 – Our appearance, grooming, and demeanor represent Capella. Our attire and personal image are appropriate and impeccable. We avoid words that are inconsistent with Capella's image, such as "hi," "ok," "no problem," "guys," etc.

#24 – As service professionals, we are always gracious and treat our guests and each other with respect and dignity.

Each team member receives a printed version of the 24 standards, known as the "Canon Card," and is expected to embody these values as they work. At the start of each shift at all Capella locations around the world, staff members meet for 15 minutes to review one of the 24 standards. On the 25th day, the cycle is repeated.

Like Capella Hotels, consider printing your core values and standards on a wallet-size card for your team members to carry around. Remind your team members of your core values at every company gathering. Perhaps even offer a $5, $10, or $20 bill to employees who can recite your company's core values on demand.

To communicate to their team the impact being made through their company visually, PHOS Creative built and mounted a wall of 267 light-bulb sockets arranged in the shape of the word "LIGHT." (In Greek, the company's name means "light.") The PHOS light wall is a way they visualize their performance in relation to their stated purpose:

To be a place team members never want to leave, clients can't do without, the world is better for, and in so doing, exemplify the love of Jesus Christ.

After each time a team member observes a moment when the company's mission was being fulfilled, they screw in a fresh lightbulb. The company's CEO said there are five things that turn on a lightbulb on the PHOS light wall:

- A new team member starting
- A new client mission partner starting with them as an agency
- A new child sponsored through Compassion International
- Someone on the team or through the agency starting their relationship with Jesus
- Anything else deemed worthy of fulfilling their mission

One of the PHOS team members said,

Once we got the light wall, it gave us a daily reminder. We come past it every morning. We get to see these little symbols of a greater mission here.[1]

PUBLICLY RECOGNIZE YOUR TEAM MEMBERS WHEN THEY DEMONSTRATE YOUR COMPANY'S CORE VALUES.

Your company's stated values won't make much of a noticeable impact on your company's culture unless you provide opportunities for your people to share and discuss examples of how they are being put into action regularly.

At High Bridge Books, our core values are 1) integrity, 2) encouragement, 3) continuous improvement, and 4) legacy. At least once per month, we devote a portion of a staff meeting to what we call "values-in-action" reports from our team members. This is a time when each team member is asked to share a recent example of a moment when he or she observed one of our fellow team members demonstrating one of our core values.

We adopted this idea from a Christ-centered manufacturing company named Polydeck who has been operating its "I Caught You Caring" program for many years as a means for team members to affirm their coworkers for modeling their company's core values. Team members who are "caught caring" for others are honored at company-wide staff meetings and given a special t-shirt.

Empower your company with a clear and Christ-centered set of core values to express your company's core purpose, and make sure it is embraced by your company's team members.

REFLECTION, DISCUSSION, AND APPLICATION

What are your company's core values? How do those values reflect aspects of God's character?

What are some other ways you can help your team members think about your core values constantly and put them into action? Which methods will you commit to implementing?

---

[1] C12 Business Forums (with PHOS Creative), "Illuminating the Marketplace," YouTube, October 19, 2021, educational video, https://www.youtube.com/watch?v=SF7E8-psedg.

Habit 5

Set Clear, Noble, and Measurable Goals

Our company pursues its mission with clear, noble, and measurable goals that are pleasing to God plus a plan of action to accomplish each of those goals.

But the noble person devises noble plans; and by noble plans he stands.

—Isaiah 32:8

The plans of the diligent lead surely to abundance.

—Proverbs 21:5a

Ponder the path of your feet; then all your ways will be sure.

—Proverbs 4:26

Therefore be careful how you walk, not as unwise men but as wise, making the most of your time, because the days are evil. So then do not be foolish, but understand what the will of the Lord is.

—Ephesians 5:15–17

G od is a meticulous planner and goal-setter. When God created the universe, he didn't rush to create everything all at once, nor did he procrastinate concerning the things that needed to get done (as we often do). As part of his mission to create humans and establish a relationship with us, he had an expressed goal for each of the seven days of Creation (Gen. 1:1-2:3) which he accomplished within a specific amount of time. God's project management system isn't a random "big bang" in which he stumbles around from task to task in a reactive mode as we tend to do. No, God's ways are part of his intelligent design, as ours should be.

Like God, we should "run in such a way, as not without aim" (1 Cor. 9:26). He will sovereignly guide us, but he wants us to "co-labor" with Him (1 Cor. 3:9) by developing and executing Christ-centered goals and plans.

Ask him what goals to set. The Holy Spirit will guide you.

What kind of goals and plans should we set?

SET NOBLE GOALS.

Isaiah said, "But the noble person devises noble plans; and by noble plans he stands" (Isa. 32:8). In this passage of Isaiah, *noble* refers to the idea of having a willing and generous heart. Such plans keep us oriented toward God and others rather than toward selfish interests.

What noble, others-centered goals have you set to move your company forward in the process of becoming a Christ-centered company? These goals should flow directly from your corporate purpose and in pursuit of your vision.

Here's an example of a noble goal set by some Christ-centered companies, including my own: "Every customer refers a new customer within one year." What makes this a noble goal?

First, a goal like this can make a direct positive impact on your customer service and operations. People will only refer people to you and your company if they have a positive experience with you. Keeping your marketing focused on faithfully serving those God has already brought to you—not just focusing on bringing in new customers—is one way to set noble goals.

Second, asking your customers for referrals is the most cost-effective way to get more customers to serve. This approach is better stewardship of your company's God-given resources than spending a bunch of money on paid advertising. Paid advertising has its place, but it's no substitute for word-of-mouth referrals from credible people who have already benefitted from your product and/or service.

Third, the focus on getting referrals from current customers will help you get more of the right kinds of customers to serve. At the time of this writing, 49 percent of the books published by my company were written by authors referred to us by other authors who had already published with us. We are looking for Christ-centered authors who want to publish a book as part of their legacy, so there's a strong probability that a prospect referred by one of our current authors will also be a Christ-centered author.

Not only should your organization's goals be noble, but they also ought to be measurable.

WHAT GETS MEASURED GETS DONE.

It will be easy to assess whether our example noble goal was accomplished. Either our new customer referred someone within the first year, or he didn't. There will be no vague perception of progress with a measurable goal like this.

If an objective isn't clear and measurable, it's not a goal. Have you ever tried to shoot a basketball into a hoop you couldn't see? There may be excuses for why the goal wasn't achieved, but at least there won't be uncertainty about what the goal was in the first place.

Proverbs instructs us, "Ponder the path of your feet; then all your ways will be sure" (Prov. 4:26). In this verse, the Hebrew word for "ponder" literally means "to weigh out" or "make level." It's not a lackadaisical wondering about how we're doing. In this verse, "pondering" means to establish clear, measurable criteria for assessing the quality and/or quantity of something.

We are only truly setting goals if we have ways to measure (i.e., "ponder") how we're progressing toward those goals. A vague desire to "grow the business" or "increase profit" won't achieve it. Whatever gets measured gets done. If it can't be measured, it's generally not getting done. How could you even know if it got "done" without having a way to measure the outcome?

MAKE A PLAN BY FOCUSING ON LEADING INDICATORS ... NOT LAGGING INDICATORS.

Financial goals are helpful, but they are usually lagging indicators of a company's performance rather than leading indicators. If you're having financial problems, those are usually just symptoms of disease within a company rather than the root cause of the disease. Likewise, strong financial indicators are usually the result of activities happening beneath the surface. The question is, *What are the activities you need to measure that will ultimately determine whether you will reach your goals?* It's helpful to have financial goals as long as you and your team spend most of your energy on improving the leading indicators that drive those financial indicators.

For example, a leading indicator for helping you ensure that "every customer refers a new customer within one year" might be to track how many times you've asked your current customers for a referral. Or you might track the average of your current customers' answers to this question over time: "On a scale of 1-10, how likely are you to recommend us to a friend?" This metric is known as a "net promoter score (NPS)."

Here's an example of how an assessment of your lagging and leading indicators can help you figure out where your focus needs to be:

- Original (unfocused) goal = Increase gross annual revenue by 20 percent

- Lagging indicator = current gross revenue, year-to-date

- Leading indicator = Number of happy customers (NPS of at least 9 or 10) today vs. same date in prior year

- New (focused) goal = Find out which of our customers have a NPS of 9 or 10, and ask 100 percent of them for a referral.

What are the leading indicators you need to be tracking to ensure you're making sufficient progress toward achieving your clear, measurable, and noble goals? As Zig Ziglar said, "If you aim at nothing, you'll hit it every time." (*In accounting-related Habits 13 and 14, we will explore this topic of performance measurement in more detail.*)

As you go through the remainder of this book, develop specific goals you and your team need to set to improve every aspect of your company.

Ask the Holy Spirit what goals your company needs to set and measure your progress toward those goals by focusing on leading indicators.

REFLECTION, DISCUSSION, AND APPLICATION

What are your "noble goals" for your company? How would the achievement of those goals reflect God's glory?

What are the leading indicators you need to track to make sure you're making sufficient progress toward those goals?

HABIT 6

FOCUS MORE ON GETTING BETTER THAN GETTING BIGGER

Our company focuses on excelling at our core focus and maximizing our current production capacity rather than focusing obsessively on growth and expansion.

For who has shown contempt for the day of small things?

—Zechariah 4:10

Let your eyes look directly ahead and let your gaze be fixed straight in front of you.

—Proverbs 4:25

You were faithful with a few things, I will put you in charge of many things.

—Matthew 25:23b

Having failed to practice "pure and undefiled religion" during the mid-first millennium B.C., Israel was forced into Babylonian captivity. During the invasion, the glorious temple built under Solomon's leadership had been destroyed. Having practiced social injustice and idolatry, Israel was found unfaithful with the Promised Land and the temple God had given to them. Their unfaithful stewardship of what God had entrusted temporarily prevented them from participating in God's blessings.

Following Israel's return to Jerusalem after their exile in Babylon, a second temple was built for God, yet the older generation was not satisfied with it. The Bible says, "The old men who had seen the first temple, *wept with a loud voice* when the foundation of this house was laid before their eyes, while many shouted aloud for joy" (Ezra 3:12b, emphasis mine). Due to their contempt for the foundations of this smaller, second temple, Israel abandoned construction of the temple for five years.

In response to those who looked upon the new temple with disdain, God questioned them, "Who despises the day of small beginnings?" (Zech. 4:10) They should have focused on honoring the Lord with what they had rather than focusing on what they didn't have.

Like the elders of Israel, have you ever been so focused on what you and your organization have not yet achieved that you began to neglect and lose sight of what God had already entrusted to you? If you're like most of us, this is an ongoing struggle. Solomon exhorts us, "Let your eyes look directly ahead and let your gaze be fixed straight in front of you" (Prov. 4:25). Stay focused on faithfully managing what God has entrusted to you today.

DEFINE YOUR CORE FOCUS AND EMBRACE GOD'S OPTIMAL GROWTH RATE FOR YOUR COMPANY.

Defining your company's core focus is your first defense against bright, shiny opportunities that can woo your and your team's attention away from the primary stewardship God has entrusted to your company. In *Good to Great*, Jim Collins refers to this core focus as a company's "hedgehog concept," which is derived from an ancient Greek parable called "The Fox and the Hedgehog." A line from the poem states, "The fox knows many things, but the hedgehog knows one big thing." Collins encourages business leaders to define a "hedgehog concept" by finding the intersection between the following:

1) What you are deeply passionate about

2) What you can be the best in the world at

3) What best drives your economic or resource engine[1]

After experiencing tremendous success in commercial painting (i.e., their *hedgehog concept*), Hasson Painting decided to enter the construction industry but shut it down within two years. Owner and CEO Bob Hasson said,

> It wasn't our niche, we weren't good at it, and we were spending way too much time on it. We had more problems with that construction division in two years than in 40 years of focusing on commercial painting. For as long as that division was active, we were off focus from our core competencies.

Stay laser-focused on delivering your core competency and value proposition to your customers. When the master in Jesus' "Parable of the Talents" returned from his journey, he said to one of the two diligent stewards,

> Well done, good and faithful slave. You were faithful with a few things, I will put you in charge of many things; enter into the joy of your master. (Matt. 25:23)

As you stay faithful in managing your core focus, watch how God increases your company's stewardship at the optimal growth rate God wants for your company. This optimal growth rate might not be as fast as you'd like it to be, but it will be better for everyone involved than growing too fast, which often results in diminished quality of service, overspending and over-hiring to keep up with the growth, and painful staffing cutbacks later.

FOCUS ON GETTING BETTER, NOT BIGGER.

Chick-fil-A's first major competitor, Boston Market (then known as Boston Chicken), was preparing to launch an aggressive growth strategy that involved opening hundreds of new restaurants. The threat posed by Boston Market became a major topic in the Chick-fil-A board and executive meetings. In a reactionary panic, Chick-fil-A's leaders began to counter Boston Market with an aggressive expansion strategy of their own. However, this strategy would require the company to take on a significant amount of additional debt.

As former Chick-fil-A Chief Marketing Officer Steve Robinson shared with me in an interview on the *Theology of Business Podcast*, Chick-fil-A's sagely founder Truett Cathy walked into the executive committee meeting at 80 years old and was asked for his thoughts on the matter. He said,

> I don't think a guy who just turned 80 years old ought to have $250 million dollars in debt on the books. Slow down. I want to get out of debt.

According to Robinson, Cathy's refusal to take on additional debt forced Chick-fil-A to live within its means and focus on getting better before getting bigger.

The focus on getting better is at the heart of making disciples. That's why the entire fast-food industry and many other industries look to Chick-fil-A as a model of quality, customer service, and innovation. In effect, Chick-fil-A is discipling the fast-food industry and beyond.

Jim Collins discovered in his research of companies that made the extraordinary leap from good to great, "Not one of the good-to-great companies focused obsessively on growth."[2] Unlike mediocre companies Collins and his team studied, the good-to-great companies focused on doing a few things extremely well. As a result, like the faithful steward in the Parable of the Talents, they were entrusted with even larger responsibilities.

Don't despise the day of small beginnings. Focus on getting better, not bigger. As you get better at your core focus, your customers will see to it that you become bigger so you can serve more of the people they care about.

REFLECTION, DISCUSSION, AND APPLICATION

What is your company's core focus?

Is it a struggle for you to focus yourself and your company's leadership team more on getting better than getting bigger?

What pace of growth is optimal for your company?

---

[1] Jim Collins, "The Hedgehog Concept," https://www.jimcollins.com/concepts/the-hedgehog-concept.html.

[2] Jim Collins, *Good to Great* (New York: HarperBusiness, 2001).

PART TWO

MARKETING, SALES, AND CUSTOMER CARE

Follow this QR code to take the
Christ-Centered Company Assessment.

HABIT 7

DEFINE AND FOCUS ON YOUR TARGET CUSTOMER

Our company has clearly defined our target customer, and we focus most of our resources on reaching and serving this target customer.

But He answered and said, "I was sent only to the lost sheep of the house of Israel."

—Matthew 15:24

... to the Jew first and also to the Greek.

—Romans 1:16

It is not those who are healthy who need a physician, but those who are sick.

—Mark 2:17a

While Jesus' mission was to reach the entire world with his message, He first focused on serving a specific group of people during the three years of his ministry on Earth: the Jewish people. Paul explains that Jesus' message came to the Jewish people first:

> For I am not ashamed of the gospel, for it is the power of God for salvation to everyone who believes, *to the Jew first* and also to the Greek. (Rom. 1:16, emphasis mine)

When a non-Jewish woman asked Jesus to heal her demon-possessed daughter, Jesus responded, "I was sent *only to the lost sheep of the house of Israel*" (Matt. 15:24, emphasis mine). Though Jesus had compassion on this Gentile woman and served her, he reminded her that she was not part of his target group. When she implored him to help her and her daughter, Jesus said, "It is not good to take the children's bread and throw it to the dogs" (Matt. 15:26). The Samaritan woman understood that the gospel message was ultimately for everybody, but she also understood Jesus was focused primarily on sharing his message with the Jewish people during his earthly ministry. Seeing she understood that the gospel was for everyone in the world, Jesus responded, "O woman, your faith is great; it shall be done for you as you wish" (Matt. 15:28).

Not only did Jesus target his message toward a specific ethnic group and nationality, the Jewish people in Israel, he targeted a specific subgroup among the Jewish people: the outcasts. Jesus said of his ministry on Earth, "I have come *to the lost sheep of the house of Israel*" (Matthew 15:24, emphasis mine). These "lost sheep" were the despised and outcast members of Israel's society, "the tax collectors and the sinners." Everything he said and did was said and done with this specific group in mind.

When Jesus invited Matthew to become one of his 12 closest disciples, Matthew held one of the most despised occupations in all of Israel, a tax collector. Tax collectors were usually affluent Jewish people who, in effect, bought the franchise rights to tax their own people on behalf of the Roman government. As long as they gave Caesar his share, they could charge their fellow Jews whatever they wanted. As a despised outcast among the Jewish people, Matthew was exactly the type of person Jesus wanted following him. The Bible says that Matthew

> … invited Jesus and his disciples to his home as dinner guests, along with many tax collectors and other disreputable sinners.

(There were *many people of this kind* among Jesus' followers.)
(Mark 2:15, emphasis mine)

During his public ministry, Jesus did not target Israel's best and brightest. He did not go after the pillars of the community. Wayward as they were, he targeted the "disreputable sinners" who epitomized the "lost sheep of the house of Israel." Insignificant as they were, these "lost sheep" were the ones who spread Jesus' message around the world.

A targeted marketing process like Jesus' is like the process of starting a bonfire. To start a bonfire, one does not light 100 matches and scatter them in random places. Instead, one needs to ignite and fan a flame upon a single, small pile of kindling wood. It may take a while to inflame the kindling, but the fire will spread by itself once that job is done. For Jesus, the lost sheep of the house of Israel were the kindling who spread his message throughout the world.

Is your company's target group as well defined as Jesus' target group?

Or are you wasting resources trying to "target" everybody?

Or perhaps you've always been untargeted in your marketing approach like almost every other small business, just sitting back and waiting to see who shows up, while proudly telling people, "We don't spend anything on marketing. All our business comes from word of mouth."

As always, Jesus' way is better.

TARGETING MAXIMIZES IMPACT RATHER THAN LIMITING IT.

As a book publisher, I have worked with many author-entrepreneurs who are afraid to target their message toward a specific group. Many of us fear that we would be "limiting" our impact by targeting a specific group. After all, wouldn't we reach a larger audience if we try to reach "everybody?" No, that is a myth rooted in fear. Ironically, products and services marketed to "everybody" usually reach very few people.

First, not everybody wants what you're offering. And that's okay.

Second, you don't have the resources to reach "everybody."

With all the noise of the Information Age competing for your prospects' attention, it has never been more important to ensure your message is targeted toward a specific, niche group of people. Today, most forms of media are available on-demand, so people can now pay attention to exactly what they want, when they want. If something is not oriented specifically for them, they are likely to ignore it.

Yes, have a massive vision, but also aim for a small target within the scope of your overall vision. Remember, as Zig Ziglar said, "If you aim at nothing, you will hit it every time." Your influence will grow as you become more specific about who you are targeting.

TARGET THOSE WHO ARE HUNGRIEST FOR WHAT YOUR COMPANY OFFERS.

Jesus said, "It is not those who are healthy who need a physician, but those who are sick" (Mark 2:17a). He did not waste his time trying to make people dissatisfied without him. Instead, he focused his time on offering solutions to people who recognized their desperation for what he was offering. Yes, Jesus loved everybody, but his approach was targeted. He pursued the outcasts, those who realized their need for him and his message. Leonard Sweet writes,

> It is clear from the Gospels that Jesus' main audience was never the religious leaders. Jesus wasn't trying to persuade or convert the Jewish establishment. Exceptions, like Nicodemus (and probably Joseph of Arimathea), came to Jesus. But Jesus was addressing the common people who gave Him a hearing. Thus He kept to the villages, staying away from the large Galilean towns, like Sepphoris and Tiberias. Interestingly, the Gospels don't mention these two cities, which were the largest in Galilee.[1]

Jesus did not waste time with people who did not recognize their need for what he was offering. When Jesus sent his disciples out to share his message, he told them, "Whoever does not receive you, nor heed your words, as you go out of that house or that city, shake the dust off your feet" (Matt. 10:14). This was not a pompous, "some-will-some-won't-so-what" attitude toward those who rejected what he was offering. He loved them, blessed them, and called his followers to do the same. He simply did not want them to waste their time with those who were not hungry for what they had to offer. He told his audiences, "He who has ears to hear, let him hear" (Mark 4:9). In other words, "My message is for those hungry for my solution."

Here are some questions to help you and your team define your company's target group:

- Who are the customers who have already paid for our products and services? Where has the revenue been coming from so far?

- What do all those customers have in common? What categories do those customers fit into?

  o If you are selling to individuals, the categories would usually be based on demographics, psychographics, geographics, etc.

  o If you are selling to organizations, the categories would likely be industry, company size, job titles of the decision-maker initiating the purchase, etc.

- Which of those customer categories has the largest representation? This will likely be your target customer.

After you've gone through this exercise, define your target customer in one or two sentences. Here are some real-world target customer examples from Christ-centered companies:

- GWT2Energy (energy management consultancy) – Decision-makers at restaurants with 50+ locations who are searching for software to improve their restaurant operations.

- Groove Life (consumer products) – Married males aged 28-45 who have kids.

- PHOS Creative (digital media) – A small- to mid-sized business in the U.S. with 10-50 employees with annual revenues of $1M+. We love working with businesses that want to create a brand system around their greater purpose, businesses that value the impact of marketing on their culture, have values that align with our own, and value digital marketing and a collaborative process, but lack the bandwidth or resources for building a comprehensive marketing team.

- High Bridge Books & Media (publishing) – Christian authors who want to leave a legacy and impact the culture through publishing their books professionally but don't have the name recognition to get a "big-name publisher" to invest a substantial amount of capital and other resources into publishing and promoting their books.

At least 80 percent of the people you contact simply won't care about what you're offering.

Another 10 percent of the people who hear your message may despise what you're offering.

The remaining 10 percent of the people who hear your message will likely want what you are offering. They will be your raving fans. They might grow to like or even love it more than you do. That 10 percent is where your company should invest at least 80 percent of its time and attention.

REFLECTION, DISCUSSION, AND APPLICATION

What type of customer is the hungriest for what you have to offer?

Are your company's sales representatives spending at least 80 percent of your time with the types of people who are hungriest for your solution? If not, what's distracting them?

In one or two sentences, how do you define your target customer?

---

[1] Leonard Sweet and Frank Voila, *Jesus: A Theography* (Nashville: Thomas Nelson, 2012), 104.

HABIT 8

ADVERTISE AND PRICE THE CUSTOMER'S OUTCOME

We advertise and price our products and services based on the positive outcomes our customers say they experience from them, and we encourage our customers to share those positive outcomes with others.

Go home to your people and report to them what great things the Lord has done for you, and how He had mercy on you.

—Mark 5:19

Now while in prison, John heard about the works of Christ, and he sent word by his disciples, and said to Him, "Are You the Coming One, or are we to look for someone else?" Jesus answered and said to them, "Go and report to John what you hear and see: those who are blind receive sight and those who limp walk, those with leprosy are cleansed and those who are deaf hear, the dead are raised, and the poor have the gospel preached to them. And blessed is any person who does not take offense at Me."

—Matthew 11:4-5

When John the Baptist was in prison, he was abysmally discouraged. John had been Jesus' chief promoter, yet while languishing there in prison depressed, he started wondering if the whole Jesus thing was just a hoax. He wondered if his cousin, friend, and Lord was merely a well-intentioned charlatan. *Had it all been for nothing?*

Jesus didn't send a message to John exhorting him to just keep the faith, rebuke the devil, and pray harder to cast out the doubt. Instead, here's the message Jesus sent back to John:

> Go and report to John what you hear and see. The blind receive sight and the lame walk. The lepers are cleansed. The deaf hear. The dead are raised. The poor have the Gospel preached to them. (Matt. 11:4)

Jesus responded with the results of what he had already accomplished rather than promises about things to come. Why did Jesus expect John not to lose heart and keep the faith? Because he gave him the proof that he had already delivered what he had promised. That's what John needed to hear, and that's what people need to hear who might be skeptical about what your company is offering in the marketplace.

Don't advertise and charge people for an aspirational outcome you merely hope your customers will experience. In your marketing and advertising, help your team members gain confidence in what your company offers by emphasizing the results rather than making unproven claims. Advertise the real-world outcomes people have experienced from your products and services. Your customers' testimonials reveal and confirm the outcomes you're truly delivering.

ASK YOUR CUSTOMERS TO SHARE WITH OTHERS WHAT YOU'VE DONE FOR THEM.

After Jesus served people, he encouraged them to go and testify to others about what he had done for them—with a few exceptions. After delivering the man possessed by a demon at Gadara, Jesus told him, "Go home to your people and report to them what great things the Lord has done for you, and how He had mercy on you" (Mark 5:19). The Bible says the man "went away and began to proclaim in Decapolis what great things Jesus had done for him; and everyone was amazed" (Mark 5:20).

At the end of his time of service on Earth, Jesus told his disciples, "You shall be My witnesses both in Jerusalem, and in all Judea and Samaria, and even to the remotest part of the earth" (Acts 1:8). Jesus commissioned them to testify to the world of everything they had seen, heard, and experienced with him.

No story is more effective as a marketing tool than the testimony of a person who has benefited from your message, product, service, or cause. Many people won't buy without first scanning the ratings and reviews for the products or services they are considering. Observing the social proof of five-star ratings and positive reviews often makes the difference in determining which product or service to buy.

However, many people won't share testimonies about you unless you ask them personally. Some people may feel they need to have your permission to talk about you and your company publicly. Go ahead and deputize them as part of your word-of-mouth marketing team. Aim to get a testimonial endorsement from the people who have already benefitted and are currently benefitting from what you're offering. Here's a portion of text we send out to our author clients periodically:

> We're looking to get some fresh testimonials to share with prospective authors who are considering publishing through High Bridge Books. Would you be willing to send us 1-3 sentences (or more) to explain to someone why they should consider working with us?

Be aggressive about getting feedback on how your product, service, cause, or message is changing lives. Archive this feedback carefully and share your positive reviews and testimonies with others.

REFLECTION, DISCUSSION, AND APPLICATION

Who are the people you need to ask for a written or video testimonial of how your company has improved their lives? What will you say to them to invite their feedback?

PROHIBIT MANIPULATIVE MARKETING TACTICS

We prohibit all manipulative marketing and sales tactics while empowering our customers with the truth necessary to make wise purchasing decisions.

A false balance is an abomination to the Lord, but a just weight is His delight.

—Proverbs 11:1

In biblical times, product packaging with standard weights was obviously not as consistent and reliable as it is today. Customers were usually at the mercy of the salesperson to weigh out the correct amounts for which they would be charged. But the accuracy of the weights used for these scales was not regulated by governmental agencies as they would be in modern marketplaces of the developed world. If you wanted to make sure you weren't being cheated, you'd better have your own scale and weights to ensure you received the full measure of what you paid for.

Unfortunately, poor people did not usually have their own scales and weights, and they were often cheated by dishonest salespeople using a "false balance," a weight on the opposing end of the scale that was lighter than it was claimed to be. God describes such a practice in business as an "abomination" (Prov. 11:1).

But His Word also says, "A just weight is His delight." God doesn't just get angry about deceitful business habits; he delights in honorable ones.

How can we delight God in our marketing and sales habits rather than performing abominations in his sight?

ERADICATE FALSE BALANCES FROM YOUR COMPANY.

Since biblical times, sales professionals have known more about a product's value, flaws, and alternatives than its prospective buyer, a phenomenon referred to as *information asymmetry*. Fortunately, the internet has empowered today's shoppers with more information and options than ever before, so this information asymmetry isn't as pronounced as it once was. But our greedy and crafty sin nature has led many sales professionals to exploit other types of "false balances" in business.

At its core, a "false balance" in a marketing or sales situation occurs when the seller deliberately withholds any part of the truth about what he is offering for the purpose of advantaging himself and disadvantaging the customer. This encompasses far more manipulation than charging different prices to different people. Here are some other "false balances" in today's marketplace:

- Advertising "limited time" offers the seller knows will still be available months from now

- Claiming a product is "award-winning" without making it clear what award(s) it won

- Claiming to be "#1 (fill in the blank)" without making it clear what that ranking is based on (e.g., claiming to be a "bestselling author" without making it clear which bestseller list the book made it on (e.g., "#1 Amazon Bestseller" is drastically smaller in scale than "#1 New York Times Bestseller")

- Suggesting that one's coaching program or online course is going to turn the purchaser's business idea into a seven-figure or eight-figure business

- Advertising a price as a special discounted "sale" price that really isn't a discount at all
- Making claims about a product's supposed health benefits that haven't been verified through clinical trials
- Intellectual property theft (e.g., plagiarism, piracy, patent infringement, trademark infringement, etc.)
- Junk fees hidden in fine print
- Predatory pricing, collusion, and price-fixing in low-competition markets
- Price signaling in which a company raises prices by about 5 percent to see if competitors will follow suit. The company will simply lower their prices if their competitors don't raise their prices in turn.
- Hyperbolic exaggerating on social media about how "people are constantly asking me for this product" when, in reality, few people are asking for it
- Fear-based advertising and selling to scare people into buying the product
- Taking/giving bribes
- Anything you or your team are doing in sales/marketing that the Lord has convicted you about

In addition to being abominable before the Lord, many of these "false balance" habits listed above are illegal forms of false advertising and could result in criminal charges.

Take an inventory of any false balances being used in your company. As with the kings of Israel whose recorded biblical legacies were based on whether they removed the "high places," centers of idolatry under their reign, it's your God-given responsibility as a leader in your company to eradicate any false balances being used to manipulate people for unrighteous gain. In God's Kingdom, a "free market" doesn't give us license to use any means necessary to get a sale.

EMPOWER YOUR CUSTOMERS WITH THE TRUTH.

No matter what or to whom we're selling, we have a God-given responsibility to educate our customers about the whole truth of what they are considering buying so they can make wise decisions on how to spend their money, time, and attention.

Although some customers don't have teachable spirits and are hellbent on learning the hard way, if you approach your customers with the heart of a teacher, many of them will give you their respect, loyalty, and patronage in exchange.

What does it look like to approach your prospects and customers with the heart of a teacher? Let's explore a few best practices in marketing and sales, "just weights" that will "delight" the Lord.

DEPRESSURIZE YOUR CUSTOMERS' SHOPPING EXPERIENCE.

While your pricing may be clear to your customers, find out if anything is being said or done to make them feel stressed or pressured when they inquire about your company's product or service offering. Start asking your customers, "Did you feel pressured to make a purchasing decision at any point when speaking with our sales associate(s)? If so, how?" Make any necessary changes based on that feedback.

If you discover that any of your sales professionals are using high-pressure or other manipulative sales tactics, put a stop to it immediately.

SET REALISTIC EXPECTATIONS.

As a book publisher, I find that many first-time authors have delusions of grandeur regarding how many books they should expect to sell. Many publishers take advantage of these unrealistic expectations and label their book publishing service offerings with grandiose terms like "The Bestseller Package," etc. To woo these authors, they conflate becoming a *New York Times* or *Wall Street Journal* bestseller over all books worldwide with becoming a bestseller on Amazon in a highly specific niche category. Amazon's rankings—which are niche-category specific—are based on sales that occurred within the past one hour, so a book can become #1 in a small category with just 30 sales in one hour. On the other hand, a book would need 9,000 different customers to purchase at least 9,000 copies within one week to become a *New York Times Bestseller*.

We explain to authors wanting their books to become *New York Times Bestsellers* that—to reach 9,000 sales from 9,000 different customers in one week—they and their book launch teams would need to send a semi-personalized email to at least 375,000 of their ideal customers on launch week, accompanied by a direct link for people to buy the book on Amazon.com, BarnesandNoble.com, or through another reputable book retailer. We certainly don't lead them to believe that simply publishing a book and doing some basic marketing is going to cause their book to become a bestseller.

In addition to clarifying what you are offering, make it clear what you are *not* offering. Eliminate any potential confusion about the outcome your customer should expect from your product or service.

MAKE YOUR PRICING CLEAR AND CONSISTENT.

In 1861, devout Christian business owner John Wanamaker—known as the "Father of Modern Advertising" and inventor of the modern department store—invented the price tag and displayed them on every product in his massive, 12-story department store in Philadelphia. Because everyone is equal before God, he believed everyone should be equal before price. He wanted people to feel welcome and comfortable in his store, not worrying about being taken advantage of by salesmen who would charge more to underinformed or passive customers. Not only did John Wanamaker recognize that "a false balance is an abomination to the Lord," he also believed the biblical promise that "a just weight is his delight."

Similarly, Flow Automotive has applied this biblical habit in the auto sales industry, an industry notorious for taking advantage of the asymmetry between what the salesman knows and what the customer knows about the value of the item under consideration for purchase. The company's owner and CEO Don Flow said,

> We did a study and found that the people who typically paid the least for the cars were the most able to pay. Those least able to pay, paid the most. For me, it was wrong to take advantage of the least able, a clear violation of the biblical mandate in the book of Proverbs.[1]

To correct this injustice in the marketplace, Flow offers "haggle-free, market-based pricing" to reduce customers' stress while car shopping.

Like Wanamaker and Flow, don't require your customers to hunt to figure out what your pricing is, and make your pricing clear and consistent from one customer to the next.

DEVELOP EDUCATIONAL CONTENT FOR YOUR CUSTOMERS.

One of my clients, GWT2energy, is a Christ-centered energy management consultancy working with some of the world's largest restaurants and retailers. As one of the foremost experts on energy management for businesses, CEO Walt Taylor is often asked for his opinion about whether solar power is a wise investment for companies to lower their energy costs. To answer this frequently asked question, he crafted a well-developed article explaining why he believes solar power is a failed technology and an unwise investment. Although his expertise and clientele put him in a prime position to capitalize on the hype related to solar power, he chooses instead to help his clients make the wisest decisions they can. In addition to saving his time from having to answer this same question repeatedly, the article he wrote now serves as a tool to educate and foster a greater sense of trust with his clients and prospective clients.

What content could your company publish (e.g., articles, video teachings, book, podcast, etc.) to empower your customers and prospective customers with the truth they need to solve the problems your company is equipped to help them solve? Give away a large portion of this content for free to educate and build goodwill with your customers. Show them your sales force consists of teachers rather than takers. Refuse to withhold any relevant truth from your customers in your sales process. A just weight is God's delight.

REFLECTION, DISCUSSION, AND APPLICATION

What are the "false balances" you see in the marketplace?

What are the "false balances" you need to eradicate from your own company?

What are some other best practices you need to implement for using "just weights" in your sales and marketing habits?

If you notice that a fellow believer's sales and marketing habits are an abomination to God, would you be willing to confront him or her about it?

---

[1] Interview with Don Flow for *Ethix*. Issue 34. April 1, 2004.
   https://ethix.org/2004/04/01/ethics-at-flow-automotive.

Habit 10

Optimize Customer Communications

Our company constantly improves our customer communications to minimize our customers' uncertainty and stress related to their purchases.

... giving no reason for taking offense in anything, so that the ministry will not be discredited ...

—2 Corinthians 6:3

Treat people the same way you want them to treat you.

—Luke 6:31

I recently purchased "trip insurance" for a hotel I booked for my wife and me. The hotel was in Key West, so it wasn't cheap. The trip insurance gave me peace of mind that the money wouldn't be wasted in the event our plans fell through for reasons beyond our control.

On the morning of our direct flight to Key West, I was notified that our flight had been canceled by the airline. We would have to wait to depart until the following day. I was comforted to know that our first night in the hotel would be covered by the trip insurance as we now had no transportation to get there on time.

Except, the "trip insurance" company refused to cover it.

After filing the claim the following week, they notified me that they wouldn't cover the hotel expense, even though the airline canceled the flight on the day of our scheduled arrival at the hotel and we had no way to get there. When I told them I felt I had been misled, they basically said, "It's in the fine print."

But this is the way bait-and-switch agreements work, and they have no place in a Christ-centered company.

BLESS YOUR CUSTOMERS WITH CLEAR, WELL-WRITTEN AGREEMENTS.

Paul writes, as much as it depends on us, we must do our best to give people "no reason for taking offense in anything, so that the ministry will not be discredited" (2 Cor. 6:3). Your business is one major aspect of your ministry in God's Kingdom and the world, so a discredit to a believer's business habits is a discredit to his Christian ministry. One of the main areas of opportunity for people to take offense in business—and, in turn, discredit whatever that company's culture represents—is when a customer's expectations for a product or service are inconsistent with what she actually received in exchange for her payment.

You can minimize offending your customers by having agreements with them that are clear, written, and well-communicated. Here are some of the benefits of "giving no reason for taking offense" through providing clear agreements to those you serve in business:

- Customers feel safe with your company because they aren't confused about what they are paying for.

- Customers understand what will happen if 1) your company doesn't fulfill its promises made in the agreement and/or 2) the customer doesn't do what he promised to do by virtue of signing the agreement.

- You'll avoid wasting your sales representatives' time having to answer questions about what the agreement is.

- You'll minimize the possibility of unpleasant surprises for the customer after the point of sale.

NEGATIVE EFFECTS OF UNCLEAR AGREEMENTS

Despite the benefits listed above, not all companies have clear, well-communicated agreements, which can result in the following negative results:

- Customers demand refunds more frequently.

- Customers may leave your company for a different one simply because the other company's contract is easier to understand.

- Possibly feeling deceived, customers may post negative ratings/reviews about your company publicly to dissuade others from doing business with you. In one way or another, they will certainly tell other people about the negative experience they had with your company.

- Your sales representatives may have to spend excessive time on the phone, online chat, etc. to explain unclear aspects of the agreement—time that could have been invested into pursuing new business.

- There's a heightened risk of being sued by upset customers. Over 40 million lawsuits are filed in U.S. state courts every year, and about half of the civil cases in state courts are contract disputes.[1]

APPLY THE GOLDEN RULE TO YOUR AGREEMENTS WITH CUSTOMERS.

As a book publisher, my clients are authors who feel a deep emotional attachment to the books they write. When they entrust the responsibility for publishing their books to my company, this is a stewardship we take seriously. For some of our authors—such as my own father, whose book we published four years before he passed away—this is one of the last major gifts they will give to their families and to the world. If we don't deliver on what we promise, in a real sense, the client's legacy is at stake.

If my team and I are ever tempted to dismiss an author's concern as petty (e.g., a seemingly trivial word change in the manuscript, etc.), we remember that the author's book is part of his legacy. That helps us to empathize with our clients and their concerns, regardless of how small or great those concerns seem to be.

Empathize with what your customers are feeling. What's at stake for your customers if your company fails to meet their expectations? Jesus taught, "Treat people the same way you want them to treat you" (Matt. 7:12a). To figure out the right way to clarify and communicate your agreements with customers, ask yourself this Golden Rule question:

> If I were the customer, what relevant truth would I appreciate knowing before agreeing to purchase this product or service, and how would I appreciate having this information communicated to me?

Here are some things you would likely want to know:

- What is the promised outcome of using this product or service as intended?

- How long will it take for me to experience this promised outcome, assuming the product/service is used as intended?

- How can I get the most value and best outcome from this product or service?

- If this product or service does not deliver the promised outcome, what will be done to make it right?

- What are the downsides of using this product or service when compared with alternative solutions?

ENSURE THE RIGHT TEAM PLAYERS UNDERSTAND THE SCOPE OF THE AGREEMENT.

I can attest to the embarrassment of promising something to a client, that client asking one of our other team members to fulfill that special request, and my team member not knowing anything about the promise that was made. This often occurs when the sales team is out of sync with the operations team responsible for delivering on the promises made by the sales team.

Make sure your operations team is always aware of and equipped to deliver on the promises made to your customers by the sales team. Make sure they have an open line of communication as these two departments can tend to clash, usually due to either 1) the sales team making promises the operations team isn't equipped to deliver on and/or 2) the operations team being unwilling to remain flexible to accommodate the desires of the customer.

USE TIERED PRICING.

When a customer wants to change the scope of a service agreement, perhaps after your team has already delivered a significant portion of the deliverables in the agreement, it may be necessary to offer tiers of service (e.g., good, better, and best options) so you can present the customer with an opportunity to upgrade to one of the higher-priced products or levels of service. Yes, we want to go the "second mile" for our customers, but we often need to charge extra to make that happen. If you're working with the right kind of customers, they will respect your need to charge extra for the additional costs incurred by your company.

OVER-COMMUNICATE THE DELIVERY STATUS OF WHAT THE CUSTOMER HAS PAID FOR.

As in every industry, some customers will request updates and answers to new questions more frequently than others during the sales and delivery processes. Other customers take more of a just-tell-me-when-it's-done-and-where-to-sign approach. Regardless of your customer's temperament, find a sustainable way to make sure the customer is always aware of what's happening, what the next step is, and when she will receive that for which she has paid.

It's better to over-communicate than to withhold helpful and reassuring truth from the customer. As in many companies, there are likely ways to automate this type of communication to conserve time on your end.

CONSIDER ALL QUESTIONS RECEIVED FROM YOUR CUSTOMERS AS OPPORTUNITIES TO IMPROVE YOUR FUTURE CUSTOMER COMMUNICATIONS.

Keep track of all the questions you are frequently asked by your customers. Each time you're asked a question, ask yourself and your team, "How can we improve our customer communications to (possibly) prevent this question from needing to be answered manually in the future?" In response to each of those questions, it may be wise to do one or more of the following:

- Update the language in your customer agreements.
- Update the language on your website, sales presentations, and other sales/marketing materials.
- Develop/update an email response template as a quick but thorough response to each question.
- Invite customers to informational webinars.
- Add a frequently asked questions (FAQ) section to your website.

REFLECTION, DISCUSSION, AND APPLICATION

What's at stake for your customers if their expectations aren't met?

Starting from the very beginning of the sales process, what are some specific things you and your team can do to minimize your customers' uncertainty and stress related to their purchase?

---

[1] Statewide Civil Caseload Composition in 26 States, 2016, https://www.courtstatistics.org/__data/assets/pdf_file/0026/23993/ewsc-2016-civil-page-2-comp-pie.pdf.

HABIT 11

GO THE "EXTRA MILE"

Our company goes the "extra mile" for our customers.

Whoever forces you to go one mile, go with him two.

—Matthew 5:41

God saw all that he had made, and it was very good.

—Genesis 1:31

Southwest Exteriors, a windows and siding company, has committed themselves to core values of love and excellence. To evaluate their commitment to these values, they ask every customer, "Did our team make you feel loved during the process?" Aside from installing windows and siding with excellence, they encourage and empower their employees to look for above-and-beyond, non-compensated ways to love their customers such as helping elderly customers with tasks around the house, carrying groceries in, assisting prospective customers who could not afford to purchase their services, and other acts of kindness that cause people to ask, "Why did you do that for me?" Southwest Exteriors team members will then share that they were motivated by the love of Jesus.[1]

The standards of Jesus are always higher than the world's standards. For example, Jesus expected his followers to carry an enemy's bags for two miles if that enemy—in their case, Roman soldiers—forced them to carry those bags for only one mile. The word "forces" in Matthew 5:41 is *angareuo*, a Persian concept for the habit of requisitioning local goods and services, especially from a conquered group of people (e.g., when Simon of Cyrene was forced by Roman soldiers to help Jesus carry his cross). The Jewish Zealots' resistance to angareuo led to the first Roman-Jewish War, accenting a significant difference between Jesus' approach to injustice from that of his Jewish contemporaries. Unlike the Zealots, Jesus encouraged his fellow Jews to view these injustices as opportunities to work for God and show they were part of a Kingdom bigger than the Roman Empire.

It would be a stretch to say we're being persecuted with angareuo in business when we're presented with opportunities to go the extra mile for our customers, team members, and other stakeholders. But our willingness to under-promise and over-deliver to exceed others' expectations in business, recognizing Jesus is on the receiving end of everything we do in business, indeed reveals whether we are of God's Kingdom or the world's.

VERY GOOD VS. GOOD ENOUGH

God doesn't make junk or defects, and he doesn't provide sloppy service. After God finished his work in the Garden of Eden, the Bible says, "God saw all that he had made, and it was very good" (Gen. 1:31). With his power working through us, he expects us to model his own spirit of excellence in our work. He never tells us to do things he's unwilling to do himself.

Evaluate the quality of the products and services you have provided over the past year. Were any areas less than "very good?" By the time you finished delivering that product or service, did it feel like you were still on the first mile? Or had you truly finished the second mile in terms of the quality you delivered?

Ask God to provide the feedback you need concerning the quality of your products and services. Allow him to set your quality standards and implement the changes he's leading you to make. In so doing, your organization will graduate from a first-mile to a second-mile company.

IT'S OKAY TO GET PAID FOR GOING THE SECOND MILE.

In a world of finite resources, someone pays the bill for second-mile efforts. If you are operating a trucking company and only factor in one out of every two miles of gas expense into your pricing, somebody still has to pay the other half of the gas expense that wasn't paid for by the customer. That's called charity, not business.

God never says or even suggests you can't be compensated financially for going the second mile for people. In a world of first-mile products and service providers, most people are eager to pay people to go the second mile for them. In some cases, they're willing to pay extravagantly.

The misguided notion that financial compensation nullifies the "second mile" aspect of a person's work is a symptom of deficient Christian theology of business and the false dichotomy between sacred and secular. If we will open our spiritual eyes to the potential for going the "second mile" in a for-profit setting—where more than 85 percent of us spend most of our waking hours—we will begin to recognize countless more opportunities to serve Jesus in our daily lives.

THE SECOND MILE DIFFERENTIATES COMPANIES.

Almost every other company in your industry only goes the first mile. This is the bare minimum needed to stay in business—at least, for the short-term.

For example, most fast-food restaurants are first-mile companies. You show up at the drive-thru, order something tasty but (usually) unhealthy, pay your money, and get your food relatively quickly (ideally with enough condiments and napkins). That's about all you would expect or hope for from a first-mile fast food restaurant.

Across the street, there's Chick-fil-A, a second-mile fast food restaurant. Company founder Truett Cathy writes,

> When customers come into Chick-fil-A, they expect to be greeted with a smile. They expect delicious food delivered quickly and accurately in a clean environment. That's the first mile—the expectation.

Second-Mile Service is about the heart, and it goes above and beyond, making sure customers get not only what they expect, but something more that makes them say "Wow!" … Almost every day we hear about a team member helping change a customer's tire or making the extra effort to return lost keys or a cell phone that was left behind. This is not a Chick-fil-A strategy, it is a way of life.

After a Correct Craft customer purchased a boat through one of Correct Craft's dealers, the dealer went bankrupt before the boat was delivered. With a legendary reputation as a God-honoring company dating back to 1925, Correct Craft made and delivered the boat even though they would never be paid for it.

Just as Jesus expects his individual followers to be distinguished as "second milers," Christ-centered companies are distinguished by their own unique versions of the second mile. What is your company's second mile that sets you apart in your market, industry, and community?

SECOND-MILE REFERRALS

If your company is unable or unwilling to deliver a particular product or service a customer wants, perhaps your "second mile" in this case is to refer the customer to a different product or service provider you trust to deliver what the customer wants.

Before we launched our own publicity service for authors in 2022, our authors had been constantly asking us how we could help them get more opportunities to talk about their books in front of new audiences. For several years, we had been referring our authors to other publicists and interview booking services to ensure our clients could receive necessary services we were not ready to provide.

We eventually developed and launched our own publicity service for our authors based on years of studying other publicists and their interactions with our clients. Rather than immediately referring everyone to other service providers, we are now able to offer affordable book publicity as a "second-mile" service to all our authors.

SECOND-MILE INNOVATIONS

Look for opportunities to innovate within the scope of your existing products and services. For Chick-fil-A, it seems their primary second-mile differentiator is that they genuinely like and respect their customers. With rare exceptions, this is typically not a sentiment most of us feel after going to other fast-food restaurants. Yes, it costs them some extra time and money to hire and train positive and respectful people in the Chick-fil-A way. But this was a relatively low-cost innovation and attitude they brought to their industry.

Second-mile innovations don't have to be complicated or expensive. Often, they are just slight improvements to your existing products and services that significantly enhance your customers' sense that you truly care about them and what they are trying to accomplish by doing business with you.

REFLECTION, DISCUSSION, AND APPLICATION

What is your primary "second-mile" differentiator that sets your company apart from the rest of your industry?

What are some new ways you can go the second mile for your customers?

---

[1] C12 Business Forums (with Southwest Exteriors), "Love and Excellence," YouTube, April 15, 2019, educational video, https://www.youtube.com/watch?v=uSO6k--q5bo.

PART THREE

ACCOUNTING AND ACCOUNTABILITY

Follow this QR code to take the
Christ-Centered Company Assessment.

HABIT 12

AVOID ETHICALLY QUESTIONABLE OPPORTUNITIES

Our company declines to engage in business opportunities that would violate our ethics.

A faithful person will abound with blessings, but one who hurries to be rich will not go unpunished.

—Proverbs 28:20

Do not be unequally yoked with unbelievers. For what partnership has righteousness with lawlessness? Or what fellowship has light with darkness?

—2 Corinthians 6:14 (ESV)

Have you ever chosen to reject a potentially lucrative business opportunity due to how it conflicted with your Christian ethics?

Akiyama Group, a biometrics technology company in Brazil,

developed the voter identification technology to automate the democratic process in Brazil. However, the process of winning that government contract was not a direct route. In the bidding process, they were pressured by government agents to engage in significant bribery or lose the business opportunity. They declined even though such corrupt behavior is standard practice in much of Brazil.

One year later, their competitor who won the bid—by diverting funds needed for the project to bribe government agents—proved unable to deliver on time or on budget. Akiyama was then awarded a late-phase reassignment of the work and achieved major recognition in the country for the excellence of their work. They also established a national brand characterized by fanatical devotion to integrity and excellence.[1]

DON'T COMPROMISE YOUR INTEGRITY.

Perhaps you've fired a client because he was disrespecting one or more of your team members.

Or maybe you declined to join forces with a potential strategic partner because doing so would result in becoming mismatched with an unbeliever whose value system is contrary to yours.

Entering contractual relationships with people who don't honor your Christian values (e.g., clients, customers, advisors, suppliers, vendors, etc.) invites bad outcomes in business. Paul writes,

> Do not be unequally yoked with unbelievers. For what partnership has righteousness with lawlessness? Or what fellowship has light with darkness? (2 Cor. 6:14)

Even if the person you're considering partnering with claims to be a believer (i.e., a born-again Christian), it's generally unwise to work with her if she obviously doesn't demonstrate that belief by upholding the same Christian values you and your team seek to promote.

When should you and your team turn down a business opportunity for ethical reasons?

DON'T DO BUSINESS WITH PEOPLE WHO DISRESPECT YOUR TEAM MEMBERS.

As with most of us, I've worked with some difficult clients during my walk with Christ in the marketplace. Before I had employees and was handling most of the daily operations that our contractors weren't handling, I would typically just grin and bear it when working with difficult clients, just thankful to have the revenue coming through the door.

As the business grew and I brought employees onboard who now handle 95 percent of the direct interactions with our clients, I had to start considering the negative toll difficult clients would take on our team members. Because they would be responsible for enduring almost all the interactions with the occasional difficult client brought onboard, I needed to start considering their feedback on the clients with whom we would choose to work.

As a team, we started praying the Lord would send us "emotionally healthy clients." Thankfully, the Lord has sent us many emotionally healthy clients (i.e., those who are, at a minimum, reasonable people) since we started praying that prayer. While a couple of our clients have been emotionally unhealthy, our team members have always been able to navigate those relationships effectively to get the job done while conducting themselves with excellence in their work and showing unmerited respect toward the client.

In one case, a client had been speaking to one of my team members with extreme disrespect and contempt in his emails to her. We had already done $10,000 of work for this client. After reviewing the correspondence between them and noting that my team member had done nothing to provoke such disrespectful and unprofessional treatment, I told the client these exact words:

> The disrespectful way you've been speaking to _____ won't be tolerated in a publishing relationship with High Bridge Books. We do have a contract in place, but you're welcome to cancel that contract and publish your book elsewhere (and take with you all the work we've done thus far) if you're unwilling to communicate without being demeaning toward my team members. It's your choice.

This client modified his behavior for a few weeks but then defaulted to his previous behavior, which made my team member's job significantly more difficult, unpleasant, and stressful. It was taking a negative toll on her even at nighttime when she wasn't working. I finally had to ask him to stop contacting her altogether and to communicate directly through me until the project had been completed.

Once we completed his project, he asked if we would be willing to work with him on publishing his next book. I declined, explaining that I couldn't subject my team members to any further disrespect from him. He then unloaded a vicious and demonic tirade of insults and baseless accusations against me the likes of which I haven't encountered in my entire adult working life.

THE CUSTOMER IS NOT ALWAYS RIGHT. CASH IS NEVER KING.

Sometimes, customers aren't just wrong; they can be rude, egotistical, and manipulative in the process, treating your team members with utter contempt. Some of them behave as though their money is intrinsically more valuable than the people who do the work for which they exchange their money, evidence of the worst kind of business theology.

If a customer ever treats one of your team members disrespectfully while your team member remains respectful and professional, refuse to do business with that customer. Protecting your team member's dignity and emotional health is far more important than whatever revenue you would lose by firing that customer.

DON'T DO BUSINESS WITH PEOPLE WHO WANT TO DO THINGS THAT ARE MORALLY WRONG.

My company, High Bridge Books, publishes books that glorify God through reaching all sorts of target audiences. This doesn't mean all of our books are Christian books written for Christians, but we do require that anything we publish will bring glory to God in some way. And we reject manuscripts from publishing if they promote values contrary to what we understand to be Christ-centered values.

For example, we have published numerous autobiographical books, which are all redemptive stories of God's power at work in a person's life. We have had to reject some of these manuscripts from publishing because they seemed to be works of revenge intended to discredit ex-spouses and other people who have offended them during their lives. Although we could have made significant revenue from some of those books, publishing non-redemptive hit pieces that don't reflect God's glory is not something we're willing to participate in.

When presented with an ethically questionable business opportunity, slow down your decision-making process. Pray about the decision, study God's Word on the matter, and seek wise counsel from other Christian brothers and sisters.

LISTEN TO YOUR GOD-GIVEN CONSCIENCE AND THE VOICE OF THE HOLY SPIRIT.

Consider how Hobby Lobby's Green family was willing to allow their entire company to be shut down simply because they refused to offer government-mandated morning-after pills as part of their employee health care policies. Such abortifacients abort a fertilized egg. Although they were fined $1.3 million per day, they refused to comply. Eventually, they won the case by a single vote at the Supreme Court.

Reject any opportunity to increase your profits by engaging in business opportunities that conflict with your conscience and what you know the Holy Spirit is leading you to do.

REFLECTION, DISCUSSION, AND APPLICATION

Have you ever turned down a business opportunity to protect your company's people, purpose, and values?

---

[1] C12 Business Forums (with Akiyama Group), "Obedience Despite Outcome," YouTube, October 27, 2021, educational video, https://www.youtube.com/watch?v=NhHiTGW1rs4.

ESTABLISH CLEARLY DEFINED INDICATORS

Our company has clearly defined indicators for evaluating the health and performance of our company.

Know the state of your flocks, and put your heart into caring for your herds.

—Proverbs 27:23

What do you think? If any man has a hundred sheep, and one of them goes astray, will he not leave the ninety-nine on the mountains, and go and search for the one that is lost? And if it turns out that he finds it, truly I say to you, he rejoices over it more than over the ninety-nine that have not gone astray.

—Matthew 18:11-13

One of Hasson Painting's foremen had an innovative idea to paint a large hotel's doors 50 to 100 at a time by setting up a spray booth in the garage under the hotel. Although the superintendent didn't like the idea at first, owner and CEO Bob Hasson said, "Let's start with 50 doors and track how much time you spend." After putting the necessary measurements in place, they learned that this new process enabled the company to speed up the process by 35 percent, a tremendous cost savings to the company.

Success can only be defined in relation to measurements that are being tracked. In biblical terms, this means you must always "know the state of your flocks." Whether your "flock" is a painting crew and 800 doors that need to be painted for a hotel, each of us has been entrusted with flocks that must be carefully managed in the most effective and efficient ways possible.

Know the State of Your Flocks.

In the Parable of the Lost Sheep (Matt. 18:11-13), Jesus suggests it is common sense for a shepherd to search for a sheep he has lost. This logic presupposes the shepherd knows how many sheep he has at all times.

How many times a day would you need to count your sheep to know whether one was missing? Throughout history, shepherds have typically counted their sheep once in the morning, once in the evening, and once after conducting any operation involving the sheep (e.g., moving the sheep from one pasture to another, shearing, tagging, foot-trimming, etc.). While "counting sheep" has become synonymous with dozing off to sleep in our modern vernacular, this process requires significant focus. One might count 20 sheep, place a mark on the ground, and then tally them by moving his hand to another mark on his crook or dropping a pebble into his pocket.[1] Each sheep must be accounted for.

What is your "flock" or "herd?" Whether we are caring for sheep or any other type of resource God has entrusted to us, Solomon reminds us, "Know the state of your flocks, and put your heart into caring for your herds" (Prov. 27:23).

How is your "flock" doing? How would you know? You can know by establishing and carefully monitoring clearly defined, relevant indicators. Indicators are standards of measurement we can use to, as Solomon said, "put our hearts into caring" for what God has entrusted to us.

KEY PERFORMANCE INDICATORS (KPIS)

Jesus reminds us that tracking only 99 percent of our stewardship isn't good enough because we will ultimately give an account for 100 percent of what God has entrusted to us. What indicators can we put in place that would enable us to track the overall health of our organizations efficiently?

Aezion Inc., a Christian-owned Texas-based custom software development company began tracking the following indicators:

- How many tasks were completed on time?

- How much rework was done on projects?

- What is the planned burn rate (i.e., rate at which a company spends money in excess of income) compared to the actual burn rate?

- How many defects are produced?

- What is our resource utilization rate?

Since implementing these types of key performance indicators across their company, Aezion's CEO reports, "We started seeing [that] customer empathy increased. And we started delivering the milestones on time."[2]

As in the case of Turbocam Group, a global turbomachinery development and manufacturing company, customers will notice when we carefully monitor the quality of work we're producing. One of Turbocam's customers, Cummins Turbo Technologies, affirmed Turbocam's commitment to excellence:

We measure delivery, quality, and cost reduction, and Turbocam is one of the highest scorers of all our suppliers for all of Cummins. They have controls in place and an infrastructure to meet and exceed our key measures and world-class performance.

Turbocam president Marian Noronha explained,

If parts need to be within a certain tolerance, we narrow the margin even more. God is our standard. We do our best by improving processes and developing our people.

Here are some examples of other indicators being tracked by other Christ-centered companies:

- What is our net profit from each product/service we sell?
- On average, how much does it cost us to get a new customer? [i.e., customer acquisition cost (CAC)]
- On average, how likely are our customers to refer us to their friends? [i.e., net promoter score (NPS)][3]
- How many proposals have we sent to prospective customers this month?
- How much revenue has been generated from new customers over the past year?
- How satisfied are our team members with their employment at our company?

To engineer and accomplish its extremely difficult transportation movements of massive equipment for its clients, Barnhart Crane and Rigging operates with a decentralized management structure through its 50 branches and over 1,700 employees. The company's Christian CEO, Alan Barnhart, explains,

> Part of our company's "secret sauce" that makes decentralization successful is the measurements utilized in the Branch Scorecard process in combination with our self-managing culture.[4]

To manage your flock well, you'll need a scorecard of key performance indicators (KPIs) that helps you and your team monitor the health of every major metric affecting your company.

REFLECTION, DISCUSSION, AND APPLICATION

What key performance indicators (KPIs) do/should you use in your company to measure the "state of your flocks?" Which are the most important for your company?

---

[1] Yan tan tethera, https://en.wikipedia.org/wiki/Yan_tan_tethera.

[2] C12 Business Forums, "Using KPIs to Faithfully Shepherd Your Business," January 7, 2021, https://www.joinc12.com/leadership/results-driven-kpis/.

[3] See Habit 31 for an explanation of net promoter score (NPS).

[4] Jeff Holler, *Bigger Than Business* (Houston: High Bridge Books, 2018), 112.

HABIT 14

STOP STUFF THAT'S NOT WORKING

We quickly establish deadlines by which underperforming areas of our company must either start producing fruit or have our company's God-given resources withheld from them.

The next day as they were leaving Bethany, Jesus was hungry. Seeing in the distance a fig tree in leaf, he went to find out if it had any fruit. When he reached it, he found nothing but leaves, because it was not the season for figs. Then he said to the tree, "May no one ever eat fruit from you again." And his disciples heard him say it. … In the morning, as they went along, they saw the fig tree withered from the roots. Peter remembered and said to Jesus, "Rabbi, look! The fig tree you cursed has withered!"

—Mark 11:12-14, 20-21

Then he told this parable: "A man had a fig tree planted in his vineyard; and he came looking for fruit on it and found none. So he said to the gardener, 'See here! For three years I have come looking for fruit on this fig tree, and still I find none. Cut it down! Why should it be wasting the soil?' He replied, 'Sir, let it alone for one more year, until I dig around it and put manure on it. If it bears fruit next year, well and good; but if not, you can cut it down.'"

—Luke 13:6-9

He cuts off every branch in me that bears no fruit, while every branch that does bear fruit he prunes so that it will be even more fruitful.

—John 15:2

According to Mark's Gospel, when Jesus was hungry and came across a fig tree that wasn't producing figs, he cursed the fig tree, causing it to wither and die. That fig tree wasn't merely unfruitful; it was wasting soil, nutrients, and water that could have been used for growing something of value. This tells us something often unnoticed about God's character: *God doesn't tolerate waste in his Kingdom.*

Building a Christ-centered company isn't just about doing more of the right habits; it's also about stopping the wrong habits. As stewards of Christ-centered companies, let's focus our God-given time and resources on "trees" that are bearing fruit rather than wasting them on things that aren't.

WHAT ARE THE "BARREN FIG TREES" IN YOUR COMPANY?

The theme for an annual issue of *Southern Weddings* was "Love Never Fails." As part of the campaign, they sold a framed artwork piece with the words "Love Never Fails" displayed in attractive gold foil lettering. The product became so successful that they launched a new line of physical products called Cultivate What Matters. The company's owner, Lara Casey, soon had to make the difficult decision to cease publication of *Southern Weddings*. This shift away from publishing the magazine enabled her to focus her and her team's time, energy, and other resources on their new venture while avoiding strain on her marriage and family and making a greater impact in the marketplace. Lara said,

> In my garden, if I have two good things growing next to each other, those roots are going to start to suck the life out of each other and suck the nutrients away from each other.[1]

Christ-centered company influencers know when to stop doing things, even good things, that will hinder them from being able to focus on what God has called them to steward. Yes, even seemingly "good" things can be the barren fig trees we need to cut down.

Barnhart Crane and Rigging used to have a policy that required managers to send thank-you notes to team members on a weekly basis. As some employees began receiving as many as four thank-you notes per week, it became clear that the initiative was being viewed by the team as merely a contrived program. As a result, it wasn't making the desired impact, so they ended the program.

Barnhart is constantly looking for areas that either need to be retooled or shut down. CEO Alan Barnhart told me,

> If we're going to add something, we have to stop doing something else. It's not necessarily that those are bad things. They're just not on our "thou shalt" list. Otherwise, you keep stacking expectations.

As the wind power industry began to dwindle in 2009, Barnhart's leaders chose to begin shutting down its division dedicated to transporting wind farm equipment, completely disbanding the division by 2012.[2] (As the market has changed in recent years, Barnhart has since renewed its focus on the wind industry.)

Here are some other real-world examples of "barren fig trees" identified and dealt with by stewards of Christ-centered companies:

- Counterproductive policies
- An underperforming team member
- An unnecessary and counterproductive level of middle management

- Pay-per-click advertising campaigns that aren't generating revenue
- An underperforming product or service
- Consultants who aren't generating results
- Ineffective technology systems

Take an inventory. What investments of time, money, and energy have you made in your company that are consistently underperforming? Which areas are distracting you and your team from what you truly need to focus on? Are there any "barren trees" in your business you've maintained for too long?

WHEN IS IT TIME TO CUT IT DOWN?

In addition to the account of Jesus literally cursing and killing off a barren fig tree recorded in Mark's Gospel, in the Gospel of Luke, Jesus tells a separate story of a fig tree that wasn't producing figs. Seeing the tree was barren, the vineyard owner in Jesus' story instructed his gardener to cut it down.

But the gardener suddenly became keen to do everything he could to help the tree produce fruit. He responded,

> "Sir, let it alone for one more year, until I dig around it and put manure on it. If it bears fruit next year, well and good; but if not, you can cut it down." (Luke 13:8-9)

Let's explore several lessons we can learn from the gardener's recommendations to the vineyard owner concerning the barren fig tree.

DO SOMETHING DIFFERENT.

First, the gardener decided to do something different than how he had previously been maintaining the fig tree. He wasn't content to rely on old methods that likely led to its poor performance in the first place. He knew he must do something different to get different results from the tree.

If your barren fig tree is worth the continued investments required for its survival and growth, how are you going to steward it differently going forward? If you keep doing what you've always done, you'll keep getting what you've always gotten.

SET A DEADLINE.

Second, he suggested that a one-year deadline be set by which the tree must either produce fruit or be cut down.

When implementing something new or trying to resurrect something that is barren in your company, give it a set amount of time to produce the desired fruit (i.e., clearly defined results). As a corollary to a phenomenon known as Parkinson's law, work shrinks to the amount of time allotted for it. Setting a deadline will help give that aspect of your business the level of focus it needs so you can adequately assess its viability.

PROTECT AND FERTILIZE.

Third, the gardener committed to digging around the tree to protect it and adding manure to fertilize it. Digging a shallow trench around the fig tree would help it to retain water. Without the trench, the water would easily wash away from the base of the tree.

If you are trying to help one of your company's "barren fig trees" produce fruit, make sure you're not siphoning other resources away from it that are vital to its performance (e.g., money, personnel, training, etc.). If the tree is truly worth keeping and maintaining, ensure sufficient resources have been allocated to fertilize it.

DON'T DELAY.

The vineyard owner asks the gardener concerning the barren tree, "Why should it be wasting the soil?" Imagine God, the owner of all things, asking you that question about the barren trees in your company. Would you immediately recognize that continuing to maintain a barren fig tree would be wasteful? Or would you be so convinced of the tree's potential that you'd establish a plan of action to revitalize it?

Saying "yes" to the wrong investments of God's resources is not a victimless crime. Saying "yes" to one thing always means saying "no" to everything else, things God may or may not have entrusted to your stewardship. The more you waste resources on barren fig trees in your company, the more you're putting your healthy trees at risk of decline, decay, and death.

If you sense the Holy Spirit is asking you to continue maintaining a barren tree while being a better steward of it than you were before, follow his lead, establish a wise plan of action, and set a deadline by which the tree must start producing sufficiently.

If God is speaking to you about barren fig trees in your company that need to be cut down, don't delay. It may be a pruning (see John 15:2) or a wholesale chopping down of something that's been wasting God's resources. Either way, it's time to start swinging that axe.

REFLECTION, DISCUSSION, AND APPLICATION

What investments of time, money, and energy have you made in your company that are consistently underperforming?

How will you decide when to stop investing in underperforming areas of your company?

---

[1] C12 Business Forums (with Cultivate What Matters), "Pruning to Grow," YouTube, February 21, 2022, educational video, https://www.youtube.com/watch?v=V-EDKYLy4PE.

[2] Jeff Holler, *Bigger Than Business* (Houston: High Bridge Books, 2018), 117.

HABIT 15

GET WISE COUNSEL

As a leader of my company, I choose to be accountable to a peer advisory group of other Christian business leaders concerning decisions affecting our company.

Where there is no guidance the people fall, but in abundance of counselors there is victory.

—Proverbs 11:14

The fear of the Lord is the beginning of wisdom, and the knowledge of the Holy One is understanding.

—Proverbs 9:10

As the new king of Israel, Rehoboam had a critical choice to make regarding whose counsel he would follow during his reign. He would either heed the counsel of the elders who served his father Solomon, or he would follow the guidance of the younger, less-experienced generation. The elders advised Rehoboam to lighten the workload and taxation Solomon had placed upon the children of Israel, but the younger men encouraged him to increase the people's burden with the misguided goal of strengthening Rehoboam's reign (1 Kgs. 12:7-10).

Tragically, Rehoboam spent too much time around the wrong people, so he heeded foolish counsel. He told the children of Israel,

> Whereas my father loaded you with a heavy yoke, I will add to your yoke; my father disciplined you with whips, but I will discipline you with scorpions. (1 Kgs. 12:10)

As a result of refusing to heed the counsel of the right people, Rehoboam's tyrannical leadership caused the united kingdom of Israel to become divided, "so Israel has been in rebellion against the house of David to this day" (1 Kgs. 12:19).

There are many advisors influencing our industries who we respect for the advice they share. The problem is most of them do not know God, nor do they share our desires to cultivate Christ-centered companies. As Larry Burkett said, "The difficulty isn't the advice they give; it's the advice they don't give, specifically, the lack of spiritual insight."[1] A diet of business advice fed primarily by advisors for whom God is categorically irrelevant will condition a person to believe that God has nothing to do with his company.

One of the primary means by which the Holy Spirit leads and protects business leaders and their organizations is godly advisors to whom the leader chooses to be accountable. Here are seven benefits you will likely experience as a result of choosing to make yourself accountable to a group of like-minded Christian business influencers:

1. Having other Christian business leaders pray for you and your company

2. Bible-based business education through cooperative dialogue

3. Christ-centered fellowship with other Christian business leaders

4. Action-oriented accountability

5. Clarified decision-making

6. A facilitator focused on your growth

7. Admonition to rely on the presence, power, and wisdom of the Holy Spirit as confirmed by God's written Word

Here are some examples of Christian peer advisory groups that offer a consistent advisory model for Christian entrepreneurs and executives where I can personally attest you will experience the benefits listed above:

- C12 Forums
- Convene Now
- Truth at Work
- Fellowship of Companies for Christ International (FCCI)
- Pinnacle Forum
- 4Word Women
- Christian Business Men's Connection (CBMC)
- The Christian CEO Institute
- G7 Networking
- Kingdom Driven Entrepreneur (KDE)
- Cornerstone Advisory Groups

I know there are more to add to this list. These are just the ones I know personally.

Leaders of Christ-centered companies give priority to the voice of counsel from those who share their Christ-centered values. God can speak to us through anybody; however, he strategically gives us access to wise advisors in our professional lives to keep us sharp, balanced, and protected from the high costs of foolishness. We will only be prepared for the next level of responsibility by having heeded the counsel of the right people.

The Bible says, "The fear of the Lord is the beginning of wisdom, and the knowledge of the Holy One is understanding" (Prov. 9:10). If you want wisdom and understanding for your business, make sure your business advisors fear, revere, and know God intimately.

REFLECTION, DISCUSSION, AND APPLICATION

Do you currently receive ongoing wise counsel and accountability from wise Christian business leaders?

Which of the "seven benefits" of joining an advisory group for Christian business leaders would be the most beneficial to you and your company right now?

---

[1] Larry Burkett, *Business by the Book* (Nashville: Thomas Nelson, 1998), 89.

HABIT 16

REPORT FINANCIAL INFORMATION HONESTLY

Our company honestly reports financial information to shareholders and to the government.

For we are taking pains to do what is right, not only in the eyes of the Lord but also in the eyes of man.

—2 Corinthians 8:21

But there was a certain man named Ananias who, with his wife, Sapphira, sold some property. He brought part of the money to the apostles, claiming it was the full amount. With his wife's consent, he kept the rest. Then Peter said, "Ananias, why have you let Satan fill your heart? You lied to the Holy Spirit, and you kept some of the money for yourself. The property was yours to sell or not sell, as you wished. And after selling it, the money was also yours to give away. How could you do a thing like this? You weren't lying to us but to God!"

—Acts 5:1-4

"Well, then," he said, "give to Caesar what belongs to Caesar, and give to God what belongs to God."

—Matt. 22:21b

Give to everyone what you owe them: Pay your taxes and government fees to those who collect them, and give respect and honor to those who are in authority.

—Romans 13:7

I once met with the church-going owner of an 18-wheeler parts remanufacturing company to explore the possibility of helping his company start selling their products online. During this exploratory meeting, I noticed they had virtually no transparency in their accounting habits. They just made sure they turned a profit on each remanufactured part; that was about it. When I asked him why they didn't use accounting software like Quickbooks, he said, "If the IRS comes in here, I'll just give them a bunch of shoeboxes full of paper they'll have to sort through. If we keep everything in a computer program like that, they'll be able to see what we're doing." He also bragged about having paid a $10,000 bribe to get a city official to overlook one of their violations. After hearing his disturbing statements and sensing he had no interest in changing his ways, I declined to work with his company.

Business accounting is the process of consolidating your company's financial information to make it clear and understandable for your stakeholders. In short, accounting is the pursuit of truth concerning your company's finances. A Christ-centered company's accounting habits must be truthful and transparent, presented without regard to how the unvarnished reality will make you look or feel.

HOW WE REPORT OUR FINANCIAL INFORMATION TO OUR STAKEHOLDERS IS HOW WE'RE REPORTING IT TO GOD.

In the Early Church, a husband and wife named Ananias and Sapphira were literally struck down by God because they gave a false account of their material possessions. Don't get the idea that their sin was only serious because, in context, they lied to a group of fellow Christian believers. Immediately before Ananias was struck dead, Peter said to him, "You weren't lying to us but to God!" (Acts 5:4) The severe consequence shows how much God hates it when Christians lie and should remind us that the Father, Son, and Holy Spirit are on the receiving end of every noble or wicked action we take in business (see Habit 1).

There is little difference between what Ananias and Sapphira did and what company leaders do when they present false financial information to their stakeholders:

- Over-reporting revenues and profits to shareholders, prospective shareholders, and prospective lenders to give them a false sense of your company's financial strength

- Hiding revenues and profits from the government to evade taxes

- Hiding revenues and profits from current lenders with the hope of delaying repayment of debts

- Over-billing clients (e.g., inflating the number of billable hours spent on a particular project)

Ultimately, God is on the receiving end of such lies.

TRUTHFULLY REPORT YOUR REVENUE AND EXPENSES TO THE GOVERNMENT.

Although I appreciate having a powerful military and police force to protect my family, I despise paying taxes when I consider how much money government officials waste through irresponsible spending. Nevertheless, just because I don't like paying taxes doesn't give me the right to misrepresent my company's revenue and expenses to the government. Paul said, "Pay your taxes and government fees to those who collect them, and give respect and honor to those who are in authority" (Rom. 13:7). If a specific law requiring tax revenue is unjust, we have the option of petitioning to change those laws, voting, running for office, etc. But we always have a responsibility before God to report our revenue and expenses to the government and other stakeholders truthfully, regardless of the outcome.

INCREASE YOUR TRANSPARENCY.

As the owner of a book publishing company, I am responsible for paying royalties to our authors for sales of 175 different books (as of this publication). After publishing our first few books, the weight of responsibility for accurately reporting each author's quarterly book sales and royalties quickly began to bear down on me. There are executives in my industry who have gone to prison for mismanaging their authors' royalties. Although none of our authors were asking for anything more than the quarterly report and payment they were receiving, I began to search for more ways to increase transparency in our financial reporting to our authors.

Before our authors come onboard with our publishing company, we give them a detailed spreadsheet that shows exactly how their royalties will be calculated, which factors in retailer fees, credit card transaction fees, and an estimate of printing cost. We also figured out a few hacks to trigger an email notification to each author every time one of his or her paperback or hardback books sold through their websites, enabling them to cross-check the sales and royalties numbers we report to them. We also educate them on how to track their Amazon book sales via their Amazon Author Central accounts. This enhanced system of transparency delights our authors.

As Paul said, "For we are taking pains to do what is right, not only in the eyes of the Lord but also in the eyes of man" (2 Cor. 8:21).

REFLECTION, DISCUSSION, AND APPLICATION

What additional "pains" should your company take to increase transparency and ensure truthful accounting habits?

PART FOUR

PEOPLE MANAGEMENT

Follow this QR code to take the
Christ-Centered Company Assessment.

HABIT 17

HIRE, PROMOTE, AND
DEMOTE BIBLICALLY

Our company hires, promotes, and demotes team members
based on a thorough assessment of their core values and
ability in relation to God's values as expressed in the Bible.

*So he shepherded them according to the integrity of his heart, and
guided them with his skillful hands.*

—Psalms 78:72

*Do you see a person skilled in his work? He will stand before kings;
He will not stand before obscure people.*

—Proverbs 22:29

*To one he gave five talents, to another, two, and to another, one,
each according to his own ability; and he went on his journey.*

—Matthew 25:15

To cultivate and protect a Christ-centered culture in your company, the Bible teaches we ought to hire people for roles that correspond with their levels of integrity, diligence, readiness, and discretion, "each according to his own ability" (Matt. 25:15). Those who lack these qualities should not be entrusted with significant influence and responsibility in our companies while those possessing them should be appointed to roles with influence and responsibility proportionate to their demonstration of those qualities.

At the same time, the primary purpose of Christ-centered companies is to disciple individuals, companies, industries, and communities. This means, as Christ-centered company influencers, we are responsible for helping to cultivate these qualities in the lives of those who work within our companies. We are called to "present every person complete in Christ" (Col. 1:28) within our spheres of influence as the Great Commission we have from Jesus is to make disciples (see Matt. 28:19), not merely to make profit.

HIRE FOR INTEGRITY.

The Bible says in Psalms 78:72 that David led God's people "according to the integrity of his heart." *Integrity* is defined as "the state of being whole, entire, or undiminished." It is an architectural term referring to the structural strength of a building. If the structure has cracks in its foundation, it won't stand over time—nor will your company stand if you hire people who lack integrity.

Those who lack integrity are likely to sow division among the team, waste and steal resources, and will certainly be counterproductive toward your efforts to cultivate a Christ-centered company. Such a person will present a poor reflection of Jesus to your customers, stakeholders, and all who encounter your company.

If a person demonstrates a breach of integrity, does it mean he should be banished from your company? If not, it certainly does mean that his integrity has been broken somehow and that, perhaps, he should be demoted to a position of lower influence where his integrity can be rebuilt within the disciple-making culture of the company.

Hire for Diligence and Readiness.

In a biblical sense, *skill* is about more than performing a particular mechanical repair, knowing how to use a complex formula in Microsoft Excel, or demonstrating another type of technical proficiency. You can show someone how to perform a particular task when she joins your team; that's the role of training. In the Bible, the term *skill* denotes capabilities deeper and more transferrable than the proficient performance of a particular task. The Bible uses two different Hebrew words for skill: *mahiyr* and *tabuwn*.

Mahiyr, the task-oriented aspect of a good team member, is used in the following proverb of Solomon:

> Do you see a man skilled [mahiyr] in his work? He will stand
> before kings; He will not stand before obscure men.
> (Prov. 22:29)

In this passage, the word *skilled* (mahiyr) is translated as "diligence and readiness in relation to one's work." This quality is essentially what Gideon was instructed to look for when selecting men to take into battle against 100,000 Midianites. God had already whittled Gideon's army down to 10,000 men, but he instructed Gideon to add another step in the hiring process.

> So he brought the people down to the water. Then the Lord
> said to Gideon, "You shall put everyone who laps the water
> with his tongue as a dog laps in one group, and everyone who
> kneels down to drink in another." Now the number of those
> who lapped, putting their hand to their mouth, was three hundred men; but all the rest of the people kneeled down to drink
> water. And the Lord said to Gideon, "I will save you with the
> three hundred men who lapped, and will hand the Midianites
> over to you; so have all the other people go, each man to his
> home. (Judg. 7:5)

With only 300 men of readiness, men who didn't drink water with their heads down like dogs, Gideon's army defeated Midian's 100,000-man army.

Have you ever worked with someone who didn't have *mahiyr*—that is, diligence and readiness in their work? I have walked into many businesses where the employees were wasting the company's time and money by surfing social media on their phones and doing other counter-productive, time-wasting activities at their employers' expense. For a time, they didn't even notice I had walked in because they were so distracted on their mobile phones. Gideon would have sent them packing.

Don't bring someone on your team who is lazy and won't work diligently when unsupervised. Demote and do not promote someone whose level of diligence and readiness to serve does not match his current level of responsibility until he can develop the level of diligence and readiness required.

HIRE FOR PRUDENCE.

Diligence isn't enough. You don't want people carrying influence and responsibilities on your team who are diligently foolish. The person you're considering hiring or promoting must also possess the kind of skillfulness attributed to David in this verse:

> ... And [David] guided them with his skillful [tabuwn] hands. (Psa. 78:72)

In this verse, the word *skillful* [tabuwn] can be translated as "understanding, discretion, prudence." We ought to hire and promote people who think wisely before they act wisely. Hire people who make prudent decisions, are thoughtful about how they relate to others, and always consider the company's values in their day-to-day decision-making concerning the company.

HIRE SLOWLY AND THOROUGHLY.

As you read these criteria for appointing leaders in the Church, you will notice that integrity, diligence, readiness, and prudence are all baked into the job requirements:

> For this reason I left you in Crete, that you would set in order what remains and appoint elders in every city as I directed you, namely, if any man is beyond reproach, the husband of

one wife, having children who believe, not accused of indecent behavior or rebellion. For the overseer must be beyond reproach as God's steward, not self-willed, not quick-tempered, not overindulging in wine, not a bully, not greedy for money, but hospitable, loving what is good, self-controlled, righteous, holy, disciplined, holding firmly the faithful word which is in accordance with the teaching, so that he will be able both to exhort in sound doctrine and to refute those who contradict it. (Titus 1:5-9)

How long would it take you to verify that a person possesses all the job requirements stated in the job description listed above? Obviously, this process will take a while; it should, and it's worth the wait. Here are a few ways you can slow down your hiring process and make it more thorough:

- Seek others' feedback about the candidate *before* hiring/promoting.
- Hire from within your company and community. This will help you profile the candidate more quickly and reliably.
- Implement a 90-day probationary period during which the candidate will be given an opportunity to meet deadlines, quality standards, etc. During this time, you will also be able to interview those who worked with the candidate directly to gain more insight about the person.
- Ask the candidate the hard, awkward questions to assess whether the candidate embraces your purpose, values, and culture.

HIRE TO MAKE DISCIPLES ... NOT MERELY PROFIT.

Where do people grow in integrity, diligence, readiness, and prudence? This happens primarily within for-profit companies as this is where almost everyone spends 60-70 percent of their waking hours. It's far more difficult to disciple someone as a follower of Christ without having some professional (and often financial) relationship with that person. This doesn't mean we can only disciple people who work with our companies, but it is much harder and less common to disciple people who don't have some level of dependence on us for their livelihood and career aspirations. For most people, a professional working relationship provides the most common context for discipleship the Lord Jesus has provided.

In 2012, Cohen Architectural Woodworking was the fastest-growing cabinet manufacturer in the United States. At the same time, approximately 60 percent of Cohen's employees were ex-convicts and/or drug addicts. Company founder Phil Cohen, a former drug addict himself, understands the need and opportunity to make disciples of Jesus in business. If you were to visit the Cohen factory in St. James, Missouri, you would meet dozens of people whose lives have been restored. Phil says, "We're not just here to build cabinets; we're here to build lives and build the families of these employees."

A child of one of the employees came up to Phil at a company cookout and said, "We have a new daddy in our house." Wives report that their husbands have been transformed for good as a result of working at Cohen Woodworking.

Journalists, reporters, and TV producers contact Phil and say, "We want to do a story about your company. We want you to tell us about your 'program.'" They assume the company is some sort of nonprofit charity organization that isn't interested in making money. Cohen certainly is providing second-chance employment; in some cases, it's third-, fourth-, and fifth-chance employment. Some of their employees' criminal sentences have been lowered simply because the local judge knew the offender was employed at Cohen Woodworking. They hire people who had just gotten out of jail the day before. The judge told one man, "If you don't get a job by Friday, you are going to jail." On Friday, Cohen hired him. They even hire people who have been convicted of extreme violence. As Phil says, they only ask that their employees "draw a hard line against their dark pasts" and start acting like the people they need to become.

Cohen Woodworking's team members are getting their lives restored, and they're also learning leadership. Those 60 percent of their employees who are ex-convicts and/or former drug addicts are not only the entry-level workers on the factory floor; Phil Cohen has discipled them as followers of Jesus and promoted some of them to high positions of leadership within the company.

We are called to "present every person complete in Christ" (Col. 1:28) within our spheres of influence as Christ-centered company influencers.

This involves hiring people for roles that correspond with their levels of integrity, diligence, readiness, and discretion, "each according to his own ability" (Matt. 25:15), and helping them to enhance those abilities and values as they work within our companies.

REFLECTION, DISCUSSION, AND APPLICATION

What qualities do you look for in the people you hire? How are those qualities consistent with God's character and values as expressed in the Bible?

What process do you use to assess a job candidate's integrity and skill (i.e., diligence, readiness, discretion, etc.), ensuring that people are hired, promoted, or demoted based on their ability?

HABIT 18

CLEARLY DEFINE FIREABLE OFFENSES

Our team members understand what offenses will result in the termination of their employment if found guilty through due process.

On the testimony of two or three witnesses every matter shall be confirmed.

—2 Corinthians 13:1

The movie *Coach Carter* tells the story of a controversial coach of an underperforming, inner-city high school basketball team made up of a group of at-risk kids. On the first day of practice, Coach Ken Carter required each player to sign a contract, agreeing to the following terms:

- Maintain a 2.3 grade-point average.
- Attend class regularly.
- Sit on the front row of all classes.
- Wear a collared shirt and tie on game days.

Although the team had won only four games during the previous season, they had remained undefeated well into Coach Carter's first season. However, when he discovered that many of his players had been sticking to their old habits of skipping their classes and settling for failing grades, he benched the entire team, canceled their games, and closed the gym until the players' grades improved to the standards they agreed to uphold on the contracts they signed at the beginning of the season.

For Coach Carter, the "bottom line" measure of success wasn't how many basketball games his team won. It was the number of his players who would get a college education and not fall deeper into the street life that had destroyed the lives of so many young men he had known.

As influencers of Christ-centered companies, our God-given commission isn't just to make a profit. It's to make disciples and cultivate a corporate culture known for helping people conduct business and life God's way. As with Coach Carter and his team, discipleship requires discipline and standards.

Regardless of your team's demographics, you can follow Coach Carter's example by establishing clear, well-communicated, and enforced agreements with your team members. The terms of these agreements should flow from the statements of core purpose and core values set for your company. Ensure each of your team members knows what it will take to remain part of the team and what could potentially get them fired.

WORKPLACE COVENANTS HAVE BIBLICAL SIGNIFICANCE.

In biblical times, two parties making a covenant would sacrifice an animal, separate it into two pieces, and walk together between the two pieces of the dead animal as to promise, "If I do not uphold my end of our agreement, let me be as this dead animal split into pieces." The message of the covenant-making ceremony reflected the grave nature of the pact.

Weinfeld asserts that the biblical Hebrew term for *covenant*, "berith," is not simply an "agreement or settlement between two parties." Instead, the term "implies first and foremost the notion of 'imposition,' 'liability,' or 'obligation.'" He proposes that the term originated from the Akkadian term, "biritu," meaning "clasp . . . fetter."[1]

Perhaps you won't be walking between two pieces of a dead animal with your new team member as part of your hiring and onboarding process, but you should have clearly written terms of your company's team covenant with him or her, including an agreement about what will happen if the covenant is not upheld by either party. Whether you or your team members realize it or not, this agreement is a covenant before God and carries spiritual significance.

WHAT WOULD GET SOMEONE FIRED FROM YOUR COMPANY?

The CEO of SonicAire, Brad Carr, brought in the Best Christian Workplaces Institute (BCWI) consultancy to evaluate the health of their company's culture. Based on the results of the surveys from all their employees, BCWI classified SonicAire's culture as toxic. Brad said,

> We had one leader who was gossiping, back-biting, and talking negatively about the other people in leadership. After four or five months of trying to work with him, it culminated when I sent him to a rather expensive 360-degree leadership week-long training course. After two days, he quit and came home, deciding he didn't need it. He didn't want to change … It was best at that point for us to part company.

After making that and other critical changes to improve the health of his company, Brad reports that SonicAire's employee engagement jumped from just 35 percent to 65 percent.[2]

Informed by your company's core purpose and core values, make a list of any covenant-breaking offenses that could get someone fired from your company. These are some items you would likely want to include:

- Consistently disrespecting customers and fellow team members
- Dishonest behavior (e.g., cheating, stealing, lying, etc.)
- Gossiping about other team members
- Abdication of work responsibilities

Once you have developed your list, write it out in statements for each team member to agree and sign. For example, the list above would become statements like these:

- I will not treat my fellow team members or customers with disrespect but will instead treat them with honor and respect.

- I will not lie, cheat, steal, or act in any other dishonest ways but will instead behave with integrity in everything I do.

- I will not gossip about any of my team members but will instead help to cultivate a workplace culture of positivity and encouragement for my team members.

- I will not abdicate any of my work responsibilities but will work with excellence in every responsibility assigned to me.

The team covenant would then include a statement like this:

I understand that, if it is proven by at least two or three witnesses that I have broken any of the terms of this team covenant, my employment may be terminated.

Why "two or three witnesses?" Because that is the biblical standard for proving someone's guilt (see Deut. 19:15; 2 Cor. 13:1; 1 Tim. 5:19). Not even the business owner is justified in firing someone without having at least two or three other witnesses to confirm whether the offense occurred. (In fact, he may face and lose a wrongful termination lawsuit with such a firing practice.) The team member would then be required to sign and date the covenant, indicating he or she understands what the fireable offenses are and what conduct will be required for continued employment.

WHAT IF THE PERSON IS REPENTANT?

If the person has broken the team covenant in some way but is sorrowful and repentant about it, should you allow him or her to remain part of the team? Maybe.

Consider how Jesus restored Peter to his position following his betrayal and subsequent repentance. Rather than demoting him from being the "Rock" upon which Jesus would build his Church, Jesus put him back in the top leadership position in his organization. This repentance and restoration is ideal but rare.

At Turbocam, an employee who has committed a significant offense against the company is given a *decision leave* without pay, which gives him one day to consider what he has done. If he returns to work the next day with an attitude of genuine remorse and repentance for what he has done, he will be able to remain employed at the company. If not, his employment is terminated.

Invite the wisdom, love, and boldness of the Holy Spirit to help you discern how to proceed if it seems you have a fallen team member who is sorrowful and repentant about what he has done. Restoring that person to his previous position could be one of the best HR decisions you ever make.

REFLECTION, DISCUSSION, AND APPLICATION

What offenses would get someone fired from your company?

Have you required each of your team members to formally acknowledge these terms?

---

[1] G.J. Botterweck and H. Ringgren, Ed., *Theological Dictionary of the Old Testament*, Vol. 2 (Grand Rapids: Eerdmans, 1975), 255.

[2] C12 Business Forums (with SonicAire), "The Tough Call for Team Health," YouTube, February 21, 2022, educational video, https://www.youtube.com/watch?v=fen5b2zovLY.

HABIT 19

ESTABLISH DECENTRALIZED MANAGEMENT

Our company's workers are expected and encouraged to make decisions at the lowest level possible.

Moses' father-in-law then said to him, "The thing that you are doing is not good. You will surely wear out, both yourself and these people who are with you, because the task is too heavy for you; you cannot do it alone."

—Exodus 18:17-18

W hile the children of Israel were camping in the wilderness during their Exodus from Egypt to the Promised Land, Moses' father-in-law Jethro came to visit him, bringing with him Moses' wife and two sons. Although he was outside of both Moses' faith and ethnicity, Jethro "rejoiced" after Moses explained to him how God had delivered and blessed the children of Israel (Exod. 18:9).

The next day was sort of a bring-your-father-in-law-to-work day as Jethro observed Moses on the job. By the end of it, Jethro was greatly disturbed by what he saw. As Moses was the only person authorized to judge legal disputes for a nation of roughly three million people, Moses' system was simply to judge as many cases as he could, by himself, from sunrise to sunset. Meanwhile, everyone else just "stands around," waiting for their turn to have their case heard (Exod. 18:14, NLT). And you think your government's services are inefficient? This was madness. Jethro said to him,

> The thing that you are doing is not good. You will surely wear out, both yourself and these people who are with you, because the task is too heavy for you; you cannot do it alone. (Exod. 18:17-18)

Jethro didn't just tell Moses the problem; he offered a two-fold solution to delegate the work, offering important lessons for those of us who have a hard time properly delegating decision-making authority.

ESTABLISH CLEAR, WRITTEN STANDARDS.

Moses could not start delegating decision-making authority until there were clear, written standards for the people to follow. Therefore, Jethro first instructed Moses to "warn them about the statutes and the laws, and make them know the way in which they must walk and what they must do" (Exod. 18:20).

Moses might have thought, "Excuse me? What laws?" God had not yet revealed the Law Moses would be responsible for teaching his people.

But Moses evidently decided to apply Jethro's advice right away, and that advice appears to have been divinely inspired. For immediately after Jethro left to go back home, Moses and the children of Israel arrived in Sinai, the site where Moses would go up on a mountaintop to receive the Law of God on tablets of stone.

Remember Capella Hotels and Resorts' 24-item "Capella Canon" from Habit 4? Consider how the language of these standards empowers their team members:

> #5 – *You are responsible* to identify and immediately correct defects before they affect a guest. Defect prevention is key to service excellence.

> #7 – Ensure all areas of the hotel are immaculate. *We are responsible* for cleanliness, maintenance, and organization.

#11 – When a guest encounters any difficulty, *you are responsible to own it* and start the problem resolution process. *You are empowered to resolve any problem* to the guest's complete satisfaction.

#19 – *We are empowered and required* to fulfill our guests' needs. Identify their unique requirements and preferences both prior to the arrival and during their stay in order to individualize their experience.

The company authorizes Capella team members to spend up to $2,000 at their own discretion to ensure these customer service standards are met.

Like Moses, before you can start delegating decision-making authority throughout your organization, you must have clear, written standards for people to follow. This will require that you document all your company's policies and processes, ensuring everyone held accountable to them knows them and can easily refer to them.

BUILD A TEAM OF CAPABLE LEADERS.

Second, Jethro advised Moses to build a team of judges to enforce the written standards taught to all the people:

> But select capable men from all the people—men who fear God, trustworthy men who hate dishonest gain—and appoint them as officials over thousands, hundreds, fifties and tens. Have them serve as judges for the people at all times, but have them bring every difficult case to you; the simple cases they can decide themselves. (Exod. 18:21-22a)

Jethro explained the benefits of this delegation plan as follows:

> That will make your load lighter, because they will share it with you. If you do this and God so commands, you will be able to stand the strain, and all these people will go home satisfied. (Exod. 18:22b-23)

Building a team of trustworthy and capable individuals would free up Moses' bandwidth so he could focus only on the most "difficult" cases, speed up the judicial process to resolve disputes faster, avoid burnout, and allow the people to have more diverse representation in their legal system. That representation would hasten the establishment of the God-centered culture the Lord wanted for Israel.

All these benefits await you and your organization if you will commit to delegating decision-making authority to the lowest level possible while ensuring the standards are clear and that "capable" people have been appointed to teach and enforce those standards.

GOD IS A DELEGATOR, AND HE LIKES TO WORK THROUGH PEOPLE.

When God created the animals, he delegated the task of naming the animals to Adam (Gen. 2:20). God brought the animals to Adam (Gen. 2:19), and Adam named them. Certainly, God could have done a far better job of naming the animals, but he chose to empower someone else with this important responsibility. God did his part and provided an opportunity for others to contribute. We are called to do the same.

John the Baptist said of Jesus, "He must increase; I must decrease" (John 3:30). How does Jesus increase? He certainly doesn't increase through our vain efforts to carry workloads too heavy for us, burning ourselves out in the process. Instead, he increases through our discipleship of other people. He increases as his followers organize, train, and equip others to share and spread his Kingdom values, message, and will throughout all of society—starting with your company.

REFLECTION, DISCUSSION, AND APPLICATION

What are some types of decisions and tasks you need to start delegating this week?

Do you have clear, written standards regarding the decision-making and tasks you need to start delegating?

Do you have capable leaders in place to teach and enforce those standards?

What are some practical ways you can cultivate a culture of delegation in your company?

HABIT 20

COMPENSATE BIBLICALLY

Our company pays our workers at least a livable wage, pays them on time, and pays most of them above market rate for their positions.

Behold, the pay of the laborers who mowed your fields, and which has been withheld by you, cries out against you; and the outcry of those who did the harvesting has reached the ears of the Lord of armies.

—James 5:4

For the Scripture says, "You shall not muzzle the ox while it is threshing," and "The laborer is worthy of his wages."

—1 Timothy 5:18

Whatever is right, I will give to you.

—Matthew 20:4

How much should we pay our team members? What is your company's overall compensation philosophy?

Quoting Leviticus, Jesus said, "The laborer is deserving of his wages" (Luke 10:7). But what should your team member's "wages" be? What are God's standards for employee compensation?

Let's start with some basic best practices and then move into some more theologically complex matters of financial compensation.

PAY ON TIME.

When Jesus says, "A laborer is worthy of his wages," it would be a stretch to interpret this as Jesus meaning, "Laborers should be paid *more* than they are currently earning." This is not really an argument for raising the minimum wage, inciting labor strikes to raise wages, etc. Instead, it seems Jesus is saying workers are worthy of the wages they *agreed to work for*. This also means those agreed-upon wages should not be withheld but should be paid promptly as the work is performed. Withholding wages was a wicked habit more common in the first century when it was easier to get away with than in modern societies, but it still happens today.

Taking advantage of people's efforts is something God takes very seriously. James rebukes employers who withhold wages, saying,

> Behold, the pay of the laborers who mowed your fields, and which has been withheld by you, cries out against you; and the outcry of those who did the harvesting has reached the ears of the Lord of armies. (James 5:4)

Regardless of the wages you and your team members have agreed upon, ensure they are paid promptly.

Does this mean employers are living up to God's standards of proper compensation by paying less than market rates as long as they pay on time? Let's explore.

PAY AT LEAST A LIVABLE WAGE.

In Matthew 20, Jesus shares a parable about a group of day laborers who were hired at various points throughout the day to work in a vineyard. Some were hired at the beginning of the day, another group at "about the third hour," other groups at "about the sixth and ninth hour," and yet another at the "eleventh hour." Although they came to work at different times, the master paid all of them a day's wage (i.e., a denarius).

The master said to the workers who went to work at the sixth and ninth hours, "Whatever is right, I will give to you" (Matt. 20:4). The master recognized that all his workers would need to keep up with their own living expenses, so he decided it would be "right" (i.e., just) to make sure they all received a full day's livable wage, regardless of what time they were hired.

DON'T EXPECT A DAY'S WORK IF YOU CAN'T OR WON'T PAY A DAY'S WAGE.

If your company simply can't afford to pay your workers at least a livable wage, make sure he or she isn't required to work with your company on a full-time basis. Don't try to turn your part-time pay into someone else's full-time livelihood. Instead, agree on a part-time work schedule and encourage your team member to get a second job, if necessary, at least until your company can afford to pay him a livable wage.

There are several resources online that can show you what an estimated livable wage amounts to on a state-by-state basis in the United States. Just Google it.

SHOULD SOME WORKERS BE PAID MORE THAN OTHERS?

Considering all the laborers were paid the same in the Parable of the Vineyard in Matthew 20, should all our workers be paid the same, regardless of the type and quality of work they do? The Parable of the Vineyard shows us there is a minimum standard of right compensation employers ought to pay, which amounts to a living wage that ensures our workers can afford their daily necessities. But the Bible has more to teach us about the issue of assigning monetary value for different types and qualities of work at different times and places.

As Christ-centered companies, it's likely that we're paying different wages to different people based on the type and quality of work they perform. But is it Christ-like to pay one person less money than another for one hour of work at the same workplace?

How should we assign monetary value to determine what a person's wages should be?

In the eyes of God, is some work more valuable than others?

Work that requires significant risk is more valuable than work that doesn't require much risk.

The statement, "No risk, no reward," is, of course, not in the Bible. However, the Bible does seem to teach that risk-taking is honored in God's Kingdom economy. Those who wisely put their time, energy, and money at risk through investing typically earn greater rewards than those who don't.

The "lazy" steward in Jesus' Parable of the Talents was "thrown to the outer darkness" for taking zero risk with the resources entrusted to him by the master in the story (Matt. 25:30). His excuse was that he was "afraid." Likewise, the average person is unwilling and often afraid to make significant investments of time, energy, and money to grow their knowledge, skills, opportunities, and professional networks. What if those investments don't pay off as they would hope? Seth Godin encourages people to approach such investments with this reality in mind: "This might not work." Work performed that might not produce the desired payoff is the kind that typically produces the greatest rewards in God's economy.

Unlike the fearful and consequently lazy steward, the two stewards who invested what they had been entrusted (i.e., risk-taking) earned back twice what they had risked in the marketplace. As such, it seems both reasonable and biblical to pay people more somewhat in proportion to the investments they have made in education and developing their knowledge, skills, opportunities, and professional networks.

Also consider the risks taken and investments made by your most loyal, longest-serving team members who have sacrificed all other professional opportunities to remain at your company exclusively and help you succeed over an extended period. These people deserve to be rewarded.

Work provided at the right time and place is more valuable than work that is not.

The Bible says, "There is a time for everything, and a season for every activity under the heavens" (Ecc. 3:1). The sons of Issachar were commended in the Bible for their ability to "discern the times and knowing what Israel should do" (1 Chron. 12:32). In business, one aspect of wisdom is offering the right high-quality products, services, and skills in the right places and at the right times.

Unfortunately, many people in today's economy have confined their skills to a specific type of job that is being displaced by new and emerging technologies. They have taken neither the steps nor made the investments necessary to find new applications for their skills. Nor have they pursued the acquisition of new skills.

It seems both reasonable and biblical to pay people who offer timely, high-quality work more than people who can only offer untimely work for which there is little-to-no demand.

Specialized/scarce work is more valuable than non-specialized work.

From the beginning, God has called people to "fill the earth, and subdue it" (Gen. 1:28). Certainly, filling the earth geographically is one aspect of fulfilling this commandment. At the same time, the earth must be filled economically as each person taps into her unique God-given abilities, cultivating ever-increasing opportunities for contributions of labor.

The 12 tribes of Israel were each given separate land inheritances so they would spread out and "fill the earth" geographically, numerically, and economically. They each became known for making different types of economic contributions. For example, when Jacob blessed his sons at the end of his life, he declared that the Tribe of Zebulun would "reside at the seashore; And he shall be a harbor for ships," referring to its calling to maritime commerce (Gen. 49:13).

In the New Testament, consider how God distributes varieties of spiritual gifts to his people through the Holy Spirit (1 Cor. 12:4-11). Nobody in the Body of Christ has the exact same mix of spiritual gifts in the exact same measures for the exact same assignments. Each person has been entrusted with a unique role in fulfilling God's mission on Earth.

We are called to be excellent in our work, but it's difficult for a generalist to be truly excellent at any specific type of work. The clear division of labor in God's economy enables us to focus on being excellent in the performance of specialized work. God didn't create people to be jacks-of-all-trades, masters-of-none. He has created and called each person to unique, specialized work although we will have multiple God-given assignments throughout our lives.

But it feels risky to specialize in a particular skill set, which is why many people don't do it.

DON'T SETTLE FOR PAYING JUST "THE GOING RATE."

Let's assume you've hired the right people who perform truly valuable work. Typically, we feel justified in paying "the going rate" for a particular line of work, but let's consider that God may be calling Christ-centered companies to exceed these cultural norms and rise to higher standards of gratitude and generosity regarding work performed by our team members.

As Jeff Van Duzer points out, the "invisible hand" of market forces Adam Smith wrote about in *The Wealth of Nations* does not necessarily equate to the sovereign hand of God. Simply because a particular labor market will bear lower wages doesn't mean higher wages shouldn't be paid by a Christ-centered company.

Consider the compensation philosophy examples set by these Christ-centered companies:

- Hobby Lobby pays all full-time workers at least twice the federal minimum wage.

- At Bridgeway Capital Management, no one can earn more than seven times the lowest paid person at the firm.

- In-N-Out pays their managers $122,011 per year on average, which is about three times the industry standard.[1]

Christians are called to be the most grateful and generous people on the planet. If that's true of us, Christ-centered company leaders would naturally want to express that greater sense of gratitude and generosity toward our team members through higher-than-average wages—and make sure they are paid in a timely manner.

REFLECTION, DISCUSSION, AND APPLICATION

What is a livable wage for your team members?

What is your company's compensation philosophy? Do you pay your team members below, at, or above the "going rate" for their work?

How do you ensure your employees, contractors, and suppliers are paid promptly for their work?

---

[1] "In-N-Out Burger salaries: How much does In-N-Out Burger pay?" https://www.indeed.com/cmp/In--n--out-Burger/salaries. Figure current as of March 3, 2023.

HABIT 21

ESTABLISH A CULTURE OF TRUST

All our team members trust each other and assume the best about each other.

---

*It [love] always protects, **always trusts**, always hopes, always perseveres.*

—1 Corinthians 13:7 NIV

D o you *love* your team members?

Do you *trust* them? That's a harder question. Isn't it?

Yet the Bible tells us love "always trusts" (1 Cor. 13:7). By that definition, do you still *love* them?

Like the oil in an engine, trust is the lubricant of delegation and getting things done in an organization. Without it, the organization's managers will operate with a suspicious attitude toward the team members, overwork, burnout, and bring down the whole organization with them.

Meanwhile, those who don't hold senior leadership positions will underperform, gossip about one another, and look for other places to work.

A business influencer who doesn't trust well carries a workload that's more than she can sustain as nobody wants to work with her, nor would she entrust the work to them anyway. She reasons within herself, *Nobody around here can do it better than me.* The overwhelming burden she carries is the weight of suspicion toward others, keeping her a prisoner of her own ego.

Yet there is one who generously trusts her team members while ensuring expectations are clear through well-defined and well-understood agreements (see Habit 18). Her trust will be exploited from time to time, but her wealth of relationships easily covers the losses and makes people eager to work with her.

In business, it's not enough to "love" your team members in the way you might love a "black sheep" member of your family or the "weak link" of your team, never believing that the person is worthy of being entrusted with anything consequential. Scottish poet George Macdonald once wrote, "To be trusted is a greater compliment than to be loved." We must trust other people with the same trust given to us by the Lord, of which we have frequently proven ourselves unworthy. Love always trusts.

DISTRUST LEADS TO POOR PERFORMANCE.

Have you ever felt distrusted? How did it make you feel? Did it strengthen your relationship and performance? Or, more likely, did it cause you to withdraw and underperform?

Consider the performance of a quarterback who doesn't trust that any of his receivers can catch a pass nor that his offensive linemen can block. The team will suffer sacks and negative yardage all day.

Consider the quality of a marriage in which the spouses don't trust each other. Zero intimacy.

Consider the performance of an employee who feels distrusted by her supervisor. She won't feel safe enough to approach her supervisor about important issues and questions on her mind, issues that will directly affect the team's performance.

We won't be able to trust God (or our team members) until we have experienced his trust in us. We cannot give what we haven't first received.

DOES GOD TRUST YOU?

My response to this question lets me know whether I'm currently feeling close to God or far from him. In fact, I'd say there is no other question you can ask a person that will more quickly and accurately reveal that person's theology and view of God. You'd probably agree that He loves you. But does God trust you?

Can God love us while simultaneously distrusting us?

Is he anticipating our next failure or our next success?

Especially in business, we usually think of trust as being only conditional. You've probably heard and thought these words at some point: "Fool me once, shame on you. Fool me twice, shame on me." As a business owner who has lost a lot of money to people who promise one thing yet do another, this is especially difficult for me.

We will not trust people simply on the basis that they deserve it. If that were the case, God wouldn't have entrusted us with anything!

A Christian business influencer who doesn't feel trusted by God would still be a child of God because he was born again into the family of God. His fellowship with God, on the other hand, would be broken. As a result, he will experience the following:

- Distrust toward God and others

- Flow of resources and outside ideas cut off

- Holy Spirit's wise counsel cut off

- Default to an orphan mentality

- Will start looking for a new "god" (e.g., approval from people, etc.) for what he needs

If you're a born-again Christian and still don't believe God trusts you, consider what God has already entrusted to you:

- Everything pertaining to life and godliness (2 Pet. 1:3)

- Every spiritual blessing in heavenly places (Eph. 1:3)

- His mission (Matt. 28:16-20)

- His Word (John 17:14)

- The earth (Gen. 1:28)

- His glory (John 17:22)
- The keys to the Kingdom of Heaven (Matt. 16:19)
- His mysteries (1 Cor. 4:1)
- The power to produce wealth (Deut. 8:18)
- A great name (Gen. 12:2)
- The temple of God (1 Cor. 6:18-19)
- His only Son (John 3:16)
- Gifts and callings (Rom. 11:29)
- Everything we have (1 Cor. 4:7)

As a born-again Christian business influencer, conduct business with the understanding that the Maker of Heaven and Earth believes you are equipped to manage faithfully what he has entrusted to you. In addition to placing your trust in God, realize he trusts you as his child and representative in the marketplace. He wants to channel his resources and ideas through you to spread the awareness of his glory throughout the world.

Although trusting other people is one of the most difficult things for a person to do, to cultivate Christ-centered companies, we must trust our team members. Let's explore a few practical ways we can grow in this essential ability.

CULTIVATE SHARED PURPOSE.

Because trust is built over time, a person must cultivate a vested interest in someone to develop trust in that person. If there's no vested interest in that person (i.e., team's success at stake, business deal at stake, department's success at stake, marriage at stake, etc.), it will be too easy for most people to abandon the relationship when times get tough. A basis for trust is the shared sense that we're on the same team, working for the same purpose. This vested interest can be established when we have shared goals with the person.

Assuming you've already established a purpose statement, core values, and goals for your team—and all team members are on board (or else they should be working somewhere else)—you already have one of the necessary ingredients to trust your team members.

CULTIVATE SHARED EXPERIENCES.

Brian Billick, coach of the 2001 Super Bowl Champions, the Baltimore Ravens, was asked about a team's chances for repeating a championship season. He replied, "It is difficult. 25 to 30 percent of the team changes every year."

Trusting a team member requires shared experiences, both positive and negative, which take time to acquire. As we gain a clear understanding of who someone is, which comes from working together with that person toward shared objectives, we develop a true bond of trust with that person. We will begin to see their strengths and flaws, allowing us to understand how we complement each other. This cultivates empathy toward that person, making it easier to overlook his flaws and focus on his strengths.

Shared experiences also help to falsify suspicions and biases we may have felt toward that person. This doesn't make us naïve about the person's flaws; it helps us gain confidence that our team member truly wants the team to win and is committed to doing his part to make that happen.

REJECT SUSPICION AND GIVE THE BENEFIT OF THE DOUBT.

When there's an opportunity to assume something negative about a person's motives, we must reject that suspicion and give our team member the benefit of the doubt. Counterproductive behavior must be questioned at face value in accordance with the social covenant you established with each team member (see Habit 18) and with the underlying assumptions that 1) the team member's motives are pure and 2) we're both committed to the success of the relationship and the achievement of our team's overall mission.

Reject a suspicious attitude toward your team members, and always assume the best about them. Trust that they want your organization to succeed just as you do. When you feel unable to trust others, draw from the endless supply of God's trust in you, never forgetting that you don't deserve it.

REFLECTION, DISCUSSION, AND APPLICATION

Do you believe God trusts you? Why or why not?

Do you trust your team members? Why or why not?

What will you commit to start doing to cultivate a deeper sense of trust in your team members?

HABIT 22

PROVIDE PASTORAL CARE TO YOUR TEAM

Our company offers pastoral care to our employees
and their families.

Bear one another's burdens, and thereby fulfill the law of Christ.

—Galatians 6:2

W ho provides pastoral care to your company's team members? I'm not asking who preaches to them on Sunday morning. I'm asking which spiritual leader is present with them as they walk through the darkest experiences and emotions of their lives. Even if most churches were great at providing this type of ministry for the people who attend their churches, according to 2020 Barna research, just 29 percent of people in the United States said they attend church at least once per week.[1] Of those, far fewer will develop close relationships at church with people who will be present and supportive when they need it most.

For nearly every adult, pastoral care will either be provided by their employers, or they won't receive it at all. Because our ultimate calling in business isn't just to make a profit but to make disciples, making sure our team members know we care about them and the difficult experiences and emotions they're walking through is a prerequisite for drawing their attention to the God we say cares about them and their loved ones. The culture of a Christ-centered company prioritizes the biblical mandate to "bear one another's burdens, and so fulfill the law of Christ" (Gal. 6:2). This is the kind of "law" Jesus is interested in, a law of love toward God and those he places in our lives (see the "new commandment" to love in John 13:34).

Here are some of the "burdens" employees haul to work with them every day which we are called to help them carry with endurance:

- Depression
- Difficult marriage
- Divorce
- Struggling children
- Caring for aging relatives
- Health issues
- Death/grief management
- Education
- Financial problems
- Loneliness
- Domestic abuse
- Addiction and/or recovery issues
- Morality and ethics related issues
- Interpersonal conflict at work
- Stress/anxiety
- Discouragement
- Faith issues[2]

EMPLOYEES' EMOTIONAL BURDENS ARE EXPENSIVE FOR COMPANIES.

The costs of employees' personal burdens to our companies are enormous, especially if nobody around our team members is gifted and qualified to minister in such circumstances. Here are some examples of these costs companies are paying:

- Dissatisfied workforce
- Absenteeism ($789 per employee per year)
- Low morale
- Safety compromises
- Turnover (2-4x salary per incident)
- Low productivity
- Theft/fraud ($4500 per employee)
- Personal conflicts (Managers spend nine weeks per year handling)
- Unhappiness
- Disengagement (Loss of $10,000 in profit annually per disengaged employee)
- Presenteeism (i.e., the habit of coming to work despite illness, injury, anxiety, etc., resulting in reduced productivity and costing businesses 10 times more than absenteeism)[3]

CONSIDER HIRING A CHAPLAIN TO SERVE YOUR COMPANY.

Some employers choose to remain in denial about what their employees are going through and take no action to help them on an emotional level. This is often because the CEO feels inadequate or awkward about providing this type of care and may conclude employees should leave their personal problems at home when they come to work. Of course, this is impossible for people to do as we aren't robots who can shut down one life experience or emotional program and start fresh on demand.

The good news is you, an influencer in your company, don't have to fulfill the chaplain role the people in your company so desperately need. You probably haven't been trained in counseling or chaplain care. Even if you have been trained, it may be difficult for your team members to be vulnerable and open up to you about the emotional and spiritual challenges they are facing. Depending on your role in the company, they may be afraid that any sensitive information they divulge about themselves may somehow be held against them by the company.

Thankfully, there are outstanding organizations like Marketplace Chaplains and Corporate Chaplains of America who already excel at providing these employee care services to companies. Offered as an employee benefit like healthcare or 401k matching, a company chaplain provides confidential counseling and a ministry of presence for employees when they need someone who truly cares about them and the challenging circumstances they are facing in their personal lives.

Regal Marine, one of the nation's largest privately owned boat building companies, annually asks its 600 employees to grade and evaluate all benefits the company offers. In one of these surveys, the Employee Care Program provided by Marketplace Chaplains was selected as their number-one favorite benefit. Mel Moses, Regal Marine's Marketing Manager said,

> The chaplains' program received the highest rating (over health insurance, retirement funding, educational scholarships, and 11 other benefits). This "highest rating" speaks loudly (from our employees).[4]

Janis K. Parker, Human Resources Manager at Hilcorp Energy Company, said this about their experience with Marketplace Chaplains:

> We love our chaplains. They are here for us at all the highs and lows in our lives. I had a chaplain who left her family at the dinner table to go to the hospital and meet with a family that had just lost a child. Our chaplains have performed celebrations and funerals for our employees and as an HR professional, it is comforting to know that—when I have an employee in the middle of an illness or tragedy, whether themselves or a family member—our Chaplain Care Team will assist them however they are needed. Even if we have a family member in another city, our chaplains will contact a chaplain in that city and send them over to be with the family. I had one employee whose mother was dying in hospice in another city, and she got the call to "come right away." While she was making travel arrangements, I was on the phone with

the chaplains, and they sent someone to sit with the mother while her daughter was en route. How cool is that?[5]

Vice President of Benefits and Compensation at Boddie-Noell Enterprises, Nanette Herbert, had this to say about how their chaplains partner with them in their mission:

> At Boddie-Noell, our motto is "We Believe in People," and partnering with Corporate Chaplains is another wonderful way to demonstrate our care and concern for our team members. Our chaplains walk alongside us with support and encouragement as we navigate the ups and downs of life. They've been there when needed for hospital visits, funerals, celebrations ... or just simply talking one-on-one with an individual. What a tremendous benefit for us all!

Jeff Brown of Corporate Chaplains of America explains why the program works:

> The program works because of three cornerstones: it is voluntary, permission-based, and confidential. Employees can opt-in or out of the program based on their choice. Also, the chaplain always asks for permission before providing any services. Finally, everything the chaplain learns from an employee is strictly confidential (legal requirements demand that someone expressing a desire to hurt themselves or someone else being the only exceptions). Employees quickly realize they can trust the chaplain, and as the employee, they determine the level and degree of care they receive from their chaplain.[6]

WHAT'S THE ROI OF HIRING A COMPANY CHAPLAIN?

Here's the best response to the chaplain-ROI question I've ever heard: "Go ask the person whose chaplain was the only person who came to the hospital when his mom died." The value of a company chaplain's ministry of presence in a team member's darkest hour is truly priceless.

But the biblical value of bearing one another's burdens has the added benefit of generating quantifiable ROI benefits as well when you invest in providing pastoral care for your team members. Wilson Lumber has retained Corporate Chaplains' services for the past 8.5 years and reports a 2.4x annual ROI on every dollar invested in chaplain services, which is comparable to financial benefits experienced by all client companies served by Corporate Chaplains and Marketplace Chaplains.

An estimated combined total of 711,000 employees and their family members are being served by Corporate Chaplains of America and Marketplace Chaplains. Combined, these chaplains are making over 3,200 worksite visits weekly. They have found that their client companies can expect to reap the following benefits as a result of hiring a company chaplain:

- Improved attitudes, teamwork, morale, and satisfaction
- Increased employee loyalty as people feel cared for and valued
- Increased commitment to goals and objectives
- Reduced employee conflicts
- Reduced stress
- Improved workplace safety
- Strengthened corporate culture
- Decreased absenteeism and presenteeism
- Increased productivity
- Reduced high turnover
- Increased employee engagement
- Enhanced spiritual/emotional wellness

In addition to achieving the benefits listed above for their client companies, Corporate Chaplains of America's 300 workplace chaplains presented the gospel message to employees and their families over 41,000 times during the year 2022.

WHAT ELSE CAN YOU DO?

Even if you feel you're not ready to invest in hiring chaplains to care for your people, there are other things you can do to help bear your team members' emotional burdens:

- Facilitate teachings and workshops for your team members regarding emotional health. For example, Correct Craft offers their team members free faith-based training to strengthen their team members' families, including seminars like *Raising Kids God's Way* and Dave Ramsey's *Financial Peace University*.

- Give your employees free subscriptions to RightNow Media @ Work, a voluntary, faith-based internet video library that offers over 5,000 videos for your employees and their family members. The collection includes content for kids plus teachings from leaders such as Patrick Lencioni, Marcus Buckingham, Zig Ziglar, John Maxwell, Les and Leslie Parrott, Dave Ramsey, and Francis Chan.[7]

- Provide a list of trusted ministries/agencies your team members can reach out to regarding a variety of issues they and/or their loved ones may be facing.

As an influencer of your company, you have a tremendous amount of spiritual responsibility for caring for the spiritual and emotional needs of your team members. As God's Word instructs us, "Bear [their] burdens, and so fulfill the law of Christ" (Gal. 6:2).

REFLECTION, DISCUSSION, AND APPLICATION

What personal burdens are your team members carrying in their personal lives?

With the influence you have, how might God want you to help bear their burdens?

[1] Barna Research, "Signs of Decline & Hope Among Key Metrics of Faith," State of the Church 2020, March 4, 2020, https://www.barna.com/research/changing-state-of-the-church/.

[2] Jason Brown, "Why Your Company Needs a Marketplace Chaplain," Center for Christianity in Business, Houston Christian University, January 26, 2018, https://hc.edu/center-for-christianity-in-business/2018/01/26/company-needs-marketplace-chaplain/.

[3] Ibid.

[4] Ibid.

[5] Ibid.

[6] Jim Brangenberg, Martha Brangenberg, and Ted Hains, *iRetire4Him: Unlock God's Purpose for Your Retirement* (Houston: High Bridge Books, 2020), 111.

[7] https://www.rightnowmedia.org/

Habit 23

Provide Rest for Your Team

Our company prioritizes rest and family time for workers by limiting work hours, ensuring every worker gets at least one day off from work each week, and providing adequate paid time off from work.

Remember the Sabbath day, to keep it holy. For six days you shall labor and do all your work, but the seventh day is a Sabbath of the Lord your God; on it you shall not do any work, you, or your son, or your daughter, your male slave or your female slave, or your cattle, or your resident who stays with you.

—Exodus 20:8-10

The Sabbath was made for man.

—Mark 2:27

Stop striving and know that I am God; I will be exalted among the nations, I will be exalted on the earth.

—Psalms 46:10

Truett Cathy, the legendary founder of Chick-fil-A, credited the tradition of staying closed on Sundays as one of the top five reasons for the success of his restaurants. Cathy said,

> I was not so committed to financial success that I was willing to abandon my principles and priorities. One of the most visible examples of this is our decision to close on Sunday. Our decision to close on Sunday was our way of honoring God and of directing our attention to things that mattered more than our business.[1]

Despite having their restaurants closed every Sunday—one of the highest-grossing days of the week for most restaurants—Chick-fil-A has had more than 47 consecutive years of sales increases, and the company's per-store sales are twice that of McDonald's.[2]

While I'm convinced God wants us and our teams to abstain from work for at least one full day each week, I'm not convinced he requires that day to be Sunday. (If that was the case, the preacher and hard-working volunteers at your church on Sunday morning would be in big trouble!) However, I do believe God's desire is that we pick a consistent day of the week and set that day apart as our Sabbath day of rest. This habit of prioritizing rest and family time should permeate the entire culture of our companies.

GOD MADE THE SABBATH FOR YOU AND YOUR TEAM.

The commandment to take a Sabbath day of rest is one of the Ten Commandments, right up there with "do not murder," "honor your father and mother," and "do not commit adultery." According to Jesus, God has not abolished any of these Ten Commandments (see Matt. 5:17).

Certainly, we are under grace and not under the Law. The sacrifice of Jesus has pardoned us from the penalty of our sins and empowered us to live holy lives. And yes, Jesus has called us to live in a state of perpetual and eternal Sabbath rest—not only on one day each week (see Heb. 4:10).

At the same time, Jesus did not abolish the fourth commandment that requires us to abstain from working for one 24-hour period each week. He knew that the practical benefits of honoring the Sabbath are too great for us and our teams to miss out on. As such, Jesus said, "The Sabbath was made for man, and not man for the Sabbath" (Mark 2:27). It's not about proving something to God or earning something from him. Taking a Sabbath day of rest is simply good for us and our teams. Even if all your team members don't buy into the biblical basis for it, it's your responsibility to cultivate a corporate culture that prioritizes rest.

Jesus said God "made" the Sabbath (Mark 2:27). Just as God made everything else on the other six days of Creation, He *made* the Sabbath day of rest on the seventh day. Rest was made *for* us and is to be managed just as we are called to manage everything else God created (see Gen. 1:28).

Here are four benefits for observing the Sabbath and cultivating a culture of rest in your company.

1 – THE SABBATH RESTORES US.

During a personal time of prayer and Bible study—back when I was a young graduate student, working full-time as a writing instructor, writing my first book, and serving in several volunteer roles—I realized I was on a path toward burnout and endless striving. Something had to change. At that pivotal time, the Holy Spirit drew my attention to this verse:

> Cease striving and know that I am God; I will be exalted among the nations, I will be exalted in the earth. (Psa. 46:10)

In response to the Lord, I decided to start taking one full day of rest from work each week. (For me, that day was Sunday.) If something felt like work, I avoided it. Given my task-oriented personality and all the time commitments I had on my schedule during that season of my life, setting aside this day of rest each week was difficult—at first. As I began to make and keep these Sunday appointments with God to relax and reflect, I began to experience the peace and clarity I had been missing in my life. On those days, I felt like an eagle, effortlessly soaring above the clouds, preparing to make my descent back into my weekly routine with a fresh and more Christ-centered perspective.

Now that I am married and have three young boys, my Sundays still mostly consist of relaxation, recreation, and reflection. And I get to enjoy it with my family. We are cultivating a culture of rest within our family, a prerequisite to establishing a culture of rest in the company I steward.

2 – THE SABBATH ENHANCES US.

Knowing I have a full day of rest, recreation, and reflection ahead on Sundays helps me to be more productive during the week. It motivates me to avoid time-wasting activities like social media browsing, excessive news reading, and doing work someone else on my team should be doing. As a result, I am more productive and effective by working six days of the week than if I worked seven days without the proper level of focus on my work.

Choosing to work only six days per week instead of seven is a practical way to invite God to "teach us to number our days, that we may gain a heart of wisdom" (Psa. 90:12). As boundaries help an artist make great art, choosing to observe the Sabbath weekly helps us and our teams to focus more on the quality of our work than its quantity.

3 – THE SABBATH CALMS US.

We have all worked with people who seem to be constantly overwhelmed, angry, and anxious. At times, that person was likely the one looking back at us in the mirror.

Taking a Sabbath day of rest is a practical way to experience the peace and strength that comes from resting in God. As discussed in Habit 2, God said to Moses, "My Presence will go with you, and I will give you rest" (Exod. 33:14). Jesus promises us, "Take my yoke upon you and learn from Me, for I am gentle and humble in heart, and you will find rest for your souls" (Matt. 11:29). When God's presence is with us, we will *find* the rest God made for us. To be sure, rest is something we must find. It won't happen unless we make it a top priority, and observing the Sabbath is a practical and measurable place to start.

4 – THE SABBATH CENTERS US.

The Sabbath is a day to focus on what matters most in our lives. Use it as an opportunity to help your team members focus on what matters most to them, which is certainly not the profitability of your company. Encourage them to completely disconnect from work on that day, reminding them not to check or send work-related emails, etc. Because the example you set shapes your company's culture, this means you shouldn't be sending work-related emails to your team members every day of the week either. Don't be a reason your team members break the fourth commandment and mismanage the rest God made for their own benefit.

Here are some practical ways you can cultivate a culture of rest in your company.

GIVE YOUR TEAM MEMBERS AT LEAST ONE DAY OFF FROM WORK EACH WEEK.

Following God's example of "making" the Sabbath for people on the seventh day of Creation, *make* rest for your people by giving them at least one day off from work each week. It will be their responsibility to manage that day of rest for its intended purpose. The Sabbath isn't just for you; it's for your team members:

> . . . on it you shall not do any work, you, or your son, or your daughter, your male slave or your female slave, or your cattle, or your resident who stays with you. (Exod. 20:10b)

ENSURE YOUR TEAM MEMBERS ARE LIMITED TO WORKING A REASONABLE NUMBER OF HOURS IN A WORKDAY.

If your team members are working 12-hour days, six days per week, what are they doing on that seventh day? Not resting—that's for sure. They're doing all the other things necessary to take care of their households which they couldn't do on the other six days (e.g., mowing the lawn, doing the laundry, paying bills, etc.). If you're expecting them to work those 12x6 workdays, make sure you're also giving them time on the clock to handle their personal matters. Don't make them wait until their Sabbath to handle all their household work.

MAKE IT EASY FOR YOUR TEAM MEMBERS TO TAKE TIME OFF.

If people need time off, they should be able to take it, assuming they're not abdicating their responsibilities in your company. They aren't indentured servants. Even if it's unpaid time off, make sure people get the time off they need to rest and take care of their personal responsibilities.

God made the Sabbath to restore, enhance, calm, and center us and our team members on what we say is most important to us. Do everything in your power to help your team manage their God-given rest well.

REFLECTION, DISCUSSION, AND APPLICATION

What policies have you implemented to cultivate a culture that prioritizes rest for yourself and your team members?

---

[1] Cathy, Truett. "Truett Cathy's Five-Step Recipe for Business Success," http://www.truettcathy.com/about_recipe.asp.

[2] Hayley Peterson, "Chick-fil-A scores more than double the sales of McDonald's per restaurant even though the chicken chain closes on Sundays," *Business Insider*, https://www.businessinsider.com/chick-fil-a-vs-mcdonalds-sales-closed-sunday-2019-7.

HABIT 24

ESTABLISH A CULTURE OF ENCOURAGEMENT

Our team members are encouraged and publicly honored much more than they are criticized.

Therefore, encourage one another and build one another up, just as you also are doing.

—1 Thessalonians 5:11

You hypocrite, first take the log out of your own eye, and then you will see clearly to take the speck out of your brother's eye.

—Matthew 7:5

It's said that most people haven't had a group of people clap for them since their high school graduation. As influencers of Christ-centered companies, we are called to cultivate cultures that "encourage one another and build one another up" (1 Thess. 5:11). At least when they're at work, our team members should be the most celebrated and affirmed people on the planet!

Physician George Adams found encouragement to be so vital that he called it "oxygen to the soul." Most people can thrive on one statement of encouragement for months. To this day, I still treasure encouraging words that were spoken and written to me many years ago. Like moths attracted to a porch light at night, we naturally move toward those who encourage us while we avoid those who discourage or withhold encouragement from us.

INSPECT YOURSELF BEFORE YOU CRITICIZE YOUR TEAM MEMBERS.

Ideally, you would have well-defined, documented processes and standards in place that will drastically reduce the amount of correcting you will need to do. If that's not true of your company, you are likely heaping discouragement upon your people unjustly when you are really the one to blame for not having clear, documented processes and standards.

As Jesus said, "First take the log out of your own eye, and then you will see clearly to take the speck out of your brother's eye" (Matt. 7:5). Before you criticize, make sure your own poor communication of your expectations isn't at the root of your team members' allegedly poor performance.

MAKE ENCOURAGEMENT YOUR DEFAULT FEEDBACK.

Industrialist Charles Schwab said, "I have yet to find the man, however exalted his station, who did not do better work and put forth greater effort under a spirit of approval than under a spirit of criticism." Nevertheless, it's tempting to criticize our team members constantly, rationalizing we are simply trying to keep them "on track." A track of discouragement is no place fitting for a human, especially not one you're expecting to perform at their highest potential.

Losada and Heaphy found that top-performing teams give each other more than five positive comments for every criticism.[1] Yes, we will have to correct our team members from time to time, but criticism shouldn't be the primary characteristic of the feedback they receive from you and the other supervisors in your company. Encouragement ought to be the main feedback they receive from influencers of a Christ-centered company.

Legendary Christian founder of Mary Kay Cosmetics, Mary Kay Ash, lived with the conviction that she and her team could "praise people to success."[2] She established a corporate culture where the default feedback given to team members is this: "Here's what you're doing right ..." Mary Kay said,

> I believe praise is the best way for a leader to motivate people.
> At Mary Kay we think praise is so important that our entire marketing plan is based on it.[3]

Likewise, legendary Christian football coach Tom Landry who led the Dallas Cowboys to 20 consecutive winning seasons and two Superbowl victories, had a policy of only showing his players footage from previous games that featured what they did *right*. He told his players, "We only re-play your winning plays," a counter-cultural approach in a sport whose coaches generally focus on what their players are doing wrong.

Don't surrender to the temptation to focus on areas in which your team members are falling short; celebrate what they're doing right. You will get more of what you draw attention to. By encouraging your team members, you are literally depositing courage inside them, enabling them to reach their highest potential.

HONOR YOUR TEAM MEMBERS PUBLICLY.

If you're looking for a good place to open a trophy shop, right outside a U.S. military base would be about as good as it gets. That's because one of the most exceptional qualities of the U.S. military's culture is its commitment to recognizing its members publicly for their achievements, both great and small. This public recognition is almost always accompanied by something tangible such as a medal, ribbon, coin, certificate, trophy, plaque, patch, pin, and/or hand-signed official letter from a senior military leader.

Aside from the highest military honors, one of the more informal yet highly valued traditions for honoring a fellow service member is through awarding a small "challenge coin" for a recent act of exemplary service. These are half-dollar-size coins military leaders of all ranks purchase as gifts of recognition for around $2-3 each, typically with their unit's logo and motto engraved on it. This simple yet powerful tool for honoring others gives them something more to reward an exceptional performance than just a handshake and an "atta boy." Commanders give these out frequently at all-hands gatherings, usually accompanied by public praise for the service member's recent remarkable deed plus a round of applause from the unit.

WHAT GETS HONORED GETS REPEATED.

When you honor your team members publicly, in addition to encouraging the person being honored, you're reminding your entire team that this is the type of behavior you want to see repeated. Whatever you honor is what gets seared into your culture as something to be highly esteemed and replicated.

GROW A CULTURE OF HONOR IN YOUR COMPANY.

Here are some questions to think through as you decide how to encourage and honor your team members consistently:

- What type of behavior should we honor? (e.g., putting one of your company's core values into action, etc.)

- What is a consistent time each week, month, etc. we should put on the schedule to honor remarkable performances publicly? (e.g., at staff meetings, etc.)

- What will we designate as our primary token of honor for the team members we publicly honor? (e.g., coin, certificate, pin, gift card, etc.)

- What tokens of honor will be given for performances deserving of greater honor? (e.g., trophy, medallion, cash, a unique/distinct gift that represents our culture, etc.)

- How will we teach our team members to cultivate a habit and lifestyle of encouraging our team members? (e.g., requiring supervisors to give at least five times as much positive feedback as negative feedback in their performance reviews, providing a public forum for team members to call out ways in which their peers have demonstrated the company's core values, writing handwritten thank-you cards, etc.)

REFLECTION, DISCUSSION, AND APPLICATION

Do the people in your company receive at least five positive comments for every one critical comment?

What could a greater culture of honor look like in your company?

---

[1] Jack Zenger and Joseph Folkman, "The Ideal Praise-to-Criticism Ratio," *Harvard Business Review*, March 15, 2013. https://hbr.org/2013/03/the-ideal-praise-to-criticism.

[2] Mary Kay Ash, *The Mary Kay Way* (Hoboken: Wiley & Sons, 2008), title of Chapter 4.

[3] Ibid., 29.

RESPECT YOUR SUPPLIERS AND CONTRACTORS

Our company treats our suppliers and contractors with respect.

For the Scripture says, "You shall not muzzle the ox while it is threshing," and "The laborer is worthy of his wages."

—1 Timothy 5:18

During the recession of the early 1990s, three general contractors represented 50 percent of Hasson Painting's annual revenue. Suddenly, those three general contractors went bankrupt within months of each other, leaving Hasson with a large amount of uncollectable revenue. That revenue was urgently needed to pay their material supplier, equipment supplier, and bonding agent for services and products rendered. Owner and CEO Bob Hasson told me in an interview for this book,

> I isolated myself from my wife and started working around the clock to figure this out, which greatly concerned my wife. She assured me, "God is going to give you a solution." And He did.
>
> I called the material supplier, equipment supplier, and bonding agent I owed money to and said, "I haven't missed

any payments, but I'm going to soon, and I need to keep getting your services. I will send you payments of [*amount confidential*] per month. As a demonstration of good faith, you'll get paid directly from our contractor so there won't be any doubt about what revenue we're receiving."

Every one of these suppliers said, "Nobody has ever come to me before a problem becomes a problem. They usually just stop responding once there's a problem."

It took me five years to pay it off. The general contractors' bankruptcies got settled, and we got paid $0.78 on the dollar—which was far better than anyone expected.

In our quest to do business God's way, perhaps the most overlooked area of our marketplace engagement as Christians concerns the way we operate as customers. This applies to both our personal shopping and to how we treat the people who supply our own companies with products and services.

In the past, customers were typically thanked for their purchases at places of business with the statement, "Thank you for your patronage." In fact, those who attend the Masters Tournament, one of the four major championships in professional golf, are still traditionally referred to as "patrons." This may sound old-fashioned, but there is rich meaning in this concept of *patronage*. The root word of "patronage," *patron*, refers to a fatherly protector of those who render products and services. When a king paid an artisan for a particular service hundreds of years ago, the king was regarded as a "patron" while the artisan was considered part of the king's patronage.

Our calling to be patrons of our suppliers and contractors—rather than exploiters—is an expression of the kingly aspect of our calling to be "royal priests" in the marketplace (see 2 Peter 1:3). In addition to being protectors (one of a king's primary roles) of our employees, co-workers, customers, etc.—as customers ourselves—we are called to protect the companies that produce and sell the products and services we buy.[1]

Let's explore some specific ways you can live out the kingly aspect of your identity as a "royal priest" through how you and your company treat your suppliers and contractors with love and respect.

PAY ON TIME.

I recently had a vendor who resells some of our books delay payment of an invoice for almost an entire year, despite frequent requests for payment. The company is significantly larger than mine, and this treatment sent the message that we simply don't matter to them. If they were a Christian-owned company and I were a non-Christian, imagine the negative impression this experience would have made or reinforced about Christians and the God they claim to serve.

Unless the supplier or contractor has volunteered to be your lender, please do not treat them as such by taking their products and services while withholding timely payment. Most companies are not in the lending business and suffer when forced to spend extra time and resources pursuing overdue payments.

> For the Scripture says, "You shall not muzzle the ox while it
> is threshing," and "The laborer is worthy of his wages."
> (1 Tim. 5:18)

Of course, if your company can't afford it, don't buy it in the first place.

DEFINE WHAT YOU'RE PAYING FOR AND WHAT YOU'RE NOT PAYING FOR.

Always be clear about the scope of what you're paying your suppliers and contractors for. If you settled for the company's low-priced "basic" option, don't expect to reap the benefits of their more expensive, "premium" option. Manage your own expectations.

If there's false advertising going on, that's a separate issue.

STOP THE ENDLESS QUEST FOR CHEAPER.

Get realistic about pricing. Cheap prices usually mean someone is getting exploited along the value chain. Those factory workers laboring for virtually nothing in an impoverished area might not be getting exploited in your own country, but somewhere, someone is often getting taken advantage of through low wages, extreme work hours, and poor working conditions.

HELP COMPANIES SAVE MONEY WHEN REASONABLE.

When companies save money, they can provide better service and stay in business longer. Below are a few examples of ways you can help your suppliers and contractors save money.

Use bank draft payments.

In certain businesses, paying with ACH bank drafts can help vendors avoid those hefty credit card transaction fees. This is the default way I pay my company's contractors, and they greatly appreciate it.

Even if it seems like the company is "big enough" to absorb the loss, aim to prevent unnecessary expenses to the company on your account. Do unto others as you would have them do unto you, even if it costs you a few credit card rewards points.

Minimize returns.

In the U.S. in 2021, approximately 16.6 percent of all purchases were returned to the store.[2] While some of these returns are the company's fault (e.g. defects, misleading descriptions, etc.), reconsider returning stuff when it's your own fault.

Read customer service information already provided.

Check the company's website and other reference sources before you pick up the phone and waste the company's time by requiring them to provide answers to questions that are readily available on the company's website and other information already provided to you.

DON'T BULLY THEIR PEOPLE.

When we pay for something, but our expectations are not met, it's tempting to unleash our frustration on the company's employees in ways that are dishonoring to God (e.g., passive-aggressive behavior, making threats, being quick to leave a 1-star rating, etc.).

When something goes wrong, calmly explain the problem. Communicate with the spiritual fruit of gentleness and the heart of a peacemaker.

BE KIND TO SALES PROFESSIONALS.

Sales professionals are faced with rejection daily at a level most of us will never experience or fully appreciate. If you're not interested in what the salesperson is offering, don't let him or her waste your time, but don't be unkind either. Politely tell the person you're not interested. Then, move on.

When you get an unwanted, spammy email or text message in your inbox, don't get angry or give a nasty reply. Simply set a filter in your inbox to prevent that person's or organization's emails from reaching your inbox. Or simply block the sender.

Genuine kindness in business is underrated and will cause people to want to know the source of your kindness, giving more people opportunities to encounter Jesus through you and your company.

PRAY BEFORE PUBLICLY SHARING A NEGATIVE REVIEW.

Several times, I have typed out a negative review for a company/product on Amazon, Google, Facebook, Yelp, etc. but then deleted it before posting. Cumulatively, these ratings and reviews can make or break a company. I restrained myself from posting the bad review because it occurred to me that I had not done enough to allow the company to resolve the issue privately.

Apply the Golden Rule when it comes to ratings and reviews. Give the company an opportunity to make it right.

GIVE CONSTRUCTIVE FEEDBACK.

If you truly want the company to succeed, let them know how they can improve. Help them get better by offering helpful suggestions for improvement.

With that said, don't be condescending or angry in how you deliver the message, or you may lose credibility, rendering your potentially helpful feedback useless.

WALK IN FORGIVENESS.

Sometimes, companies will simply disregard our grievances. What then? First, forgive before taking further action. See Habit 28.

PRAISE YOUR SUPPLIERS PUBLICLY.

Our theology of business is revealed, in part, by our level of gratitude for the people who provide our products and services in the marketplace. Unfortunately, it never occurs to most of us to write a public review for a company unless it's about something negative. Right now, consider posting a kind rating and review for one of your suppliers or contractors who has been making your company better.

Be a Christ-centered customer. Be a patron with the protective heart of God, helping your suppliers and contractors succeed so they can continue providing value for your company and the other people they serve. Let them see Jesus in your company.

REFLECTION, DISCUSSION, AND APPLICATION

How quickly do you pay your company's suppliers and contractors?

Do your company's suppliers and contractors feel respected by your company? Why or why not?

Do you have any strained relationships with any of your company's suppliers or contractors? Have you contributed to the strain on the relationship? How could you reconcile with them?

How could you express your gratitude for one of your suppliers or contractors today?

---

[1] Darren Shearer, *The Marketplace Christian* (Houston: High Bridge Books, 2015). See Chapter 2 for more on this subject of our kingly and priestly roles as marketplace Christians.

[2] Melissa Repko, "A more than $761 billion dilemma: Retailers' returns jump as online sales grow," CNBC.com, https://www.cnbc.com/2022/01/25/retailers-average-return-rate-jumps-to-16point6percent-as-online-sales-grow-.html.

PART FIVE

BUSINESS LAW & CONFLICT

Follow this QR code to take the
Christ-Centered Company Assessment.

HABIT 26

PURSUE PEACE

Our team members pursue peace when conflicts arise, confront directly when there's an offense, and have zero tolerance for gossip.

Blessed are the peacemakers, for they will be called sons of God.

—Matthew 5:9

If possible, so far as it depends on you, be at peace with all people.

—Romans 12:18

... but speaking the truth in love, we are to grow up in all aspects into Him who is the head, that is, Christ.

—Ephesians 4:15

What's the first thing that comes to mind when you think about business law? Lawyering up? See you in court? Getting even? An eye for an eye?

Packaging Technology Group's (PTG) top customer, a multi-billion-dollar international company, illegally gave away PTG's patented technology and process information to one of PTG's competitors to get a lower price on their products and services. When he discovered the theft, PTG owner Bill Blezard immediately consulted the Lord in prayer regarding what course of action to take and sought wise counsel from his C12 peer group of fellow Christian business owners. Rather than taking legal action through the courts, Bill chose a path of reconciliation and restitution. He said,

> The Lord was saying to me to "be still" … The Bible says we're supposed to be peaceable. We're supposed to seek to walk in unity with people as best we can.

Once the offending company's executives received Bill's letter about the violation, they realized they had been caught red-handed. They quickly flew Bill to their headquarters, eager to discuss and resolve the matter before it became public.

When Bill arrived, he was greeted by one of the senior executives. As they began to discuss their families, the executive mentioned that his daughter-in-law had recently given birth to a child with an extremely rare disease that only affects one out of 1.5 million people. Bill said,

> Immediately, it impacted me because I am the father of a special needs son. I couldn't care what we were there for because God was all over me. All I could think about was ministering to this man. I knew at that moment during the meeting that it was God's hand. I still stand in awe.

Bill soon discovered that this senior executive's granddaughter had been born with mucopolysaccharidosis disease, the same rare disease with which Bill's son had been born. Bill said, "Not only did God show up for ministry, but God also restored the relationship just because He can … just because that's who He is."[1]

Jesus said, "Blessed are the peacemakers, for they shall be called sons of God" (Matt. 5:9). When conflict arises in business, regardless of who is at fault, that's our opportunity to make peace and prove ourselves to be sons and daughters of God. Peacemaking ought to define a Christian's approach to business law and conflict.

When Jesus said, "Blessed are the *peacemakers*" —the act of cultivating peace where it is absent—he was not telling us merely to be *peacekeepers*.

He knows strife and injustice are rampant in business and everywhere else people have competing interests. Attempting to "keep the peace," a form of denial and conflict avoidance, usually results in increased strife and injustice as conflicts over-pressurize and eventually explode. The only way to prevent this from happening is to *make* peace deliberately. As David admonishes us, "Seek peace and pursue it" (Psa. 34:14b).

JESUS: THE PRINCE OF PEACE

Isaiah prophesied of Jesus that he would be the "Prince of Peace" (Isa. 9:6). When you want to make peace in a particular business conflict, the first practical step is to invite the Prince of Peace into the conflict. He has walked into far worse than whatever you're facing, and he would eagerly accept the challenge of establishing a fountainhead of peace amid your dispute, no matter how big or small. Invite him in, even if the other party isn't interested in doing so. He will send his Holy Spirit to make peace through you, his appointed peacemaker.

SOME PEOPLE WON'T ACCEPT PEACE.

Paul writes, "*If possible,* so far as it depends on you, be at peace with all people" (Rom. 12:18, emphasis mine). One implication of this verse is that, sometimes, it's not possible to be at peace with certain people. For a variety of reasons that stem from our original sin nature and its desires of the flesh, some people are simply hostile and unwilling to live in peace. The Bible says one of the "six things the Lord hates" is "a person who stirs up conflict in the community" (Prov. 6:19, NIV). Of course, nobody is out of reach from God's grace and mercy on this side of eternity, but when people reject peace, they are rejecting Jesus, the Prince of Peace.

Regardless of how the other party responds, God expects us to do everything we can, through the power of his Holy Spirit, to make peace with the other party in the conflict. This includes people we may want to pursue legal action against and even people who may be pursuing legal action against us.

PROHIBIT GOSSIP AND REQUIRE YOUR TEAM MEMBERS TO CONFRONT DIRECTLY.

Gossiping occurs when one discusses a problem with someone who is neither part of the problem nor the solution. When an offense occurs, many people are unwilling to confront the offender directly, especially when the offender is a coworker with whom they'll be working consistently. The fear of an awkward conversation and potentially finding out there is more to the story prevents them from having a conversation that could make peace in your company.

So what do they do instead? In need of validation and someone to agree with their selfish and biased verdict about the situation, they gossip to their other coworkers about the person who offended them. In his book *Relactional Leadership*, Ford Taylor—former CEO of a $300 million sportswear company—writes,

> Nearly every time [a person is about to gossip], the person will say, "I'm just seeking your counsel."
>
> To which, I reply, "Well, I happen to have that person's number right here in my phone. Why don't we just call that person right now so you can share with him (or her) what you just shared with me?" Even if I don't have the other person's number in my phone, I do give the counsel to go talk to that person and not talk to others.
>
> You would be amazed by how little actual gossip I hear now and how often I can be part of the solution if someone does come to me. They still come for counsel, but they know I will tell them to go talk to the other person after that counsel. That is being part of the solution.[2]

In Matthew 18, we are instructed to go directly to those who have offended us. If you and your team members will go directly to your offenders with a forgiving and humble heart, the conflict will likely be resolved right away. Whether they are Christians or not, make sure your team members know this is the only acceptable way to handle a conflict with another team member in the company.

And make it absolutely clear to your team members that zero gossip will be tolerated. Cut off this escape route for those who want to avoid confronting directly or simply letting it go. If you hear someone gossiping about a team member, customer, supplier, vendor, or anyone else, shut it down. Or that gossip cancer will spread and destroy the peace in your company. The person listening to the gossip without challenging the approach is just as guilty as the gossiper unless he or she is directly involved in the conflict as part of the problem or the solution.

MAKE PEACE ... WHEN IT'S THE OTHER PERSON'S FAULT.

Hasson Painting once had a manager fire an entire work crew of commercial painters and tell them they were "pieces of $ percent!#." CEO Bob Hasson said,

> When I heard what that manager said, I confronted him immediately and asked, "Do you like working with us?"
>
> The manager said, "Oh, yeah! I've never been treated this well by a company I've worked for!"
>
> Bob asked, "Do we treat you with respect?"
>
> The manager replied, "Oh, absolutely!"
>
> Bob then asked him, "Then, who gave you permission to tell our employees they were pieces of $ percent!#? You need to call every one of them and apologize right away. If you do this again, you won't be working here.

Bob started personally mentoring that manager as a leader in his company. Having experienced a change of heart and habits, that manager is still working with Hasson Painting 25 years later.

The Bible teaches us, "But *speaking the truth in love*, we are to grow up in all aspects into Him who is the head, that is, Christ" (Eph. 4:15, emphasis mine). This verse has often been interpreted as primarily meaning, "I should tell that person the truth because I love him." Yes, we should always tell people the truth, but when it's to our advantage to speak the truth, most of us have no hesitation to speak it. Where we typically go wrong is in *how* we speak the truth, which is one of the main issues being addressed in Ephesians 4:15. The "in love" aspect especially refers to the kind of attitude we ought to have when speaking the truth.

What is our attitude when speaking the truth when someone else is at fault? Are we quick to anger? Disrespectful? Dismissive? Yes, speak the unvarnished truth about what the other person did. But when confronting him who is at fault, speak the truth with a loving attitude of kindness, gentleness, and compassion.

MAKE PEACE ... WHEN IT'S YOUR FAULT.

When it's your fault, be quick to apologize. In *Relactional Leadership*, Ford Taylor suggests using the following six-step apology:

Step 1: State the offense. State aloud to the other person what he or she believes you did to him or her. Say, "You are right. I did _____. I did that." If you have to qualify your apology by saying, "If I did _____," it's not a real apology.

Step 2: Acknowledge that you were wrong. Use these three simple words: "I was wrong."

Step 3: Apologize. It's very simple. Say, "I am sorry." Remember not to say, "I want to tell you that I am sorry" or "I want to apologize." These are not apologies. They are statements that you "want to" but are not going to.

Step 4: Ask for forgiveness. Ask, "Will you forgive me?" It doesn't matter what the person's answer is. They don't have to say "yes" or "no," but it is important that you ask. Once you have asked, you have done your part. Regarding the relationship, the next step is now entirely up to the other person.

Step 5: Ask for accountability. Tell the person who you hurt, "I give you permission to hold me accountable for not behaving this way anymore."

Step 6: Ask if there's anything else. Ask the person, "Is there anything else I've done in our relationship that I need to apologize for?" When you ask that, you're going to surprise the other person.[3]

In addition to using the six-step apology yourself, be sure to teach this peacemaking tool to your entire team. Most people never learned good peacemaking skills growing up, so don't leave this to chance. Let them know that, going forward, this is how each of you need to apologize when at fault.

At Flow Motors, the peacemaking process is based on truth and grace. The process involves bringing the conflicting parties together in one room and offering them space for apology and forgiveness. A facilitator follows a five-step process that emphasizes the following:

1. Teaching the peacemaking principles
2. Coaching parties to follow principles
3. Counseling individuals when they are not able to ask forgiveness
4. Disciplining behaviors that contravene company standards
5. Terminating employees who are not encouraging a culture of peace

How will you and your team members pursue peace when conflict inevitably arises?

REFLECTION, DISCUSSION, AND APPLICATION

When conflict arises in your company, do you and your team members generally pursue peace?

What is your response when you hear gossip in your company?

How should you and your team members confront when at fault?

How should you and your team members confront when the other person is at fault?

[1] C12 Business Forums (with SonicAire), "A Resolve for Restoration," YouTube, May 20, 2020, educational video, https://www.youtube.com/watch?v=0yv19OrfhmE&t=9s

[2] Ford Taylor, *Relactional Leadership* (Houston: High Bridge Books, 2017), 66.

[3] Ibid., 47-49.

HABIT 27

COMPENSATE WRONGED CUSTOMERS

Our company compensates customers sufficiently when they have been wronged.

But Zaccheus stopped and said to the Lord, "Behold, Lord, half of my possessions I am giving to the poor, and if I have extorted anything from anyone, I am giving back four times as much." And Jesus said to him, "Today salvation has come to this house, because he, too, is a son of Abraham."

—Luke 19:8-9

Come to good terms with your accuser quickly, while you are with him on the way to court, so that your accuser will not hand you over to the judge, and the judge to the officer, and you will not be thrown into prison.

—Matthew 5:25

Have you ever failed to deliver on something you promised to your customer?

When I published the first book through my company, High Bridge Books, the first 1000 copies were printed with about 40 percent of the pages having faded ink. I was positive it was the printer's fault.

But it wasn't. It was my fault.

The book was a compilation of devotionals from the author's blog, and they had all been copied and pasted from the author's website and then organized, categorized, edited, and branded to form a complete manuscript. Unfortunately, about 40 percent of that copied-and-pasted text was only 95 percent black and was never changed to 100 percent black; on a computer screen, there isn't a noticeable difference between 95 percent black text and 100 percent black text. However, in a printed book, the difference is stark.

I couldn't tell the author, "Well, at least people can still read it." I couldn't say, "Well, Mr. Author, you approved the proof copy when it looked just like that."

Here's what I did say: "The error was 100 percent my fault, and I'm going to make it right. I will replace all the books at no cost to you."

Having wronged a customer is especially hard when you were initially sure it was someone else's fault, when you have excuses for why other people share some of the blame, and when you will have to pay so much recompense money that it's going to hurt badly. In my case, it cost me thousands of dollars to make it right with my first client.

I couldn't have guaranteed myself that this client would want to do business with me again simply because I tried to make it right. However, I was sure I'd lose a lot of sleep until I did.

Thankfully, this particular author has now published five books through our company and has been one of our website and social media clients on retainer for eight consecutive years. You'd probably agree I wouldn't have enjoyed this long-term relationship with this client if I hadn't admitted my error and compensated him accordingly.

WHAT'S THE RIGHT RECOMPENSE FOR A WRONGED CUSTOMER?

When *we* are at fault, we are expected to offer more than an apology, depending on the severity of the wrongdoing.

Consider how Jesus commended Zaccheus, a repentant tax collector who previously had been extorting his own people for the benefit of himself and Israel's enemies, for his willingness to offer recompense to those he wronged both directly and indirectly. The Bible says,

> Zaccheus stopped and said to the Lord, "Behold, Lord, half of my possessions I will give to the poor, and if I have defrauded anyone of anything, I will give back four times as much." (Luke 19:8)

Jesus didn't say, "Oh, Zach, there's no need for that. You're being too hard on yourself. You're under grace, not under law."

Instead, Jesus said to him,

> Today salvation has come to this house, because he, too, is a son of Abraham. For the Son of Man has come to seek and to save that which was lost. (Luke 19:9)

You and your company probably haven't extorted anyone on a regular basis like Zacchaeus did. But it's likely that you've failed to deliver on some aspect of a promise you've made to a customer at some point. Jesus advises us,

> Come to good terms with your accuser quickly, while you are with him on the way to court, so that your accuser will not hand you over to the judge, and the judge to the officer, and you will not be thrown into prison. (Matt. 5:25)

Whether the person you and your company wronged is angry about it or not, you owe him. Settle it quickly before it escalates.

The principle of "an eye for an eye" means the recompense ought to be proportionate to the wrongdoing (see Deut. 19:21). Your first responsibility is to determine the impact of the wrongdoing upon the customer. Consider the following factors:

- Was the customer warned about the potential risks in advance?
- Was the customer partially at fault?

- Was your company solely at fault?
- Was one of your suppliers or contractors partially at fault?

If it is agreed that there is shared responsibility for a costly error, consider proposing that the financial responsibility should be shared proportionately between the parties responsible.

Seeking to determine the right recompense can be difficult, so it's best to invite counsel from a third party such as your peer advisory group (see Habit 15) or from a Christian legal expert (see Habit 29).

OFFER A SATISFACTION GUARANTEE.

Groove Life, a $50 million Christian-owned consumer products company based in Franklin, Tennessee, offers a 93-year warranty on their products. This is just one example of their radical commitment to customer satisfaction after the sale. Groove Life CEO Peter Goodwin said,

> Most people stop wowing the customer at purchase. That's when you have to double-down on WOW because that's when they expect it to stop.[1]

Flow Automotive teaches its team members that their relationship with their customers should be considered as a sacred covenant. As such, they have dedicated their dealerships and repair shops as "a place that keeps its promises and is worthy of their [customers'] trust."[2] As an expression of this dedication, Flow takes pride in its "fix it right the first time" service guarantee policy, which states the following:

> We guarantee to fix your car right the first time or you don't pay! You'll never pay additional repairs associated with the original problem.[3]

When Flow sells a pre-owned vehicle, they back that vehicle with a powertrain warranty up to 100,000 miles, a three-day money-back guarantee, and two years of free maintenance. Flow will pick up the car and drop it back off to avoid any inconvenience to the customer.

COMPENSATE WRONGED CUSTOMERS

Although such promises are certainly good pre-sale promotion, making a covenant like this with your customers should be far more than an advertising gimmick. Customers should, at least, get what they paid for and be compensated fairly when they don't. Before they start working with you, let them know this is your commitment to them. More importantly, deliver on that promise of compensation in those rare instances when your customer's expectations aren't met or exceeded.

REFLECTION, DISCUSSION, AND APPLICATION

What's an example of a time you were wronged by a company? Did that company make it right? If so, how?

What's an example of how your company failed one of your customers? How did you (or should you) make it right?

What new policies does your company need to implement to ensure customers are compensated fairly when wronged?

---

[1] C12 Business Forums (with Groove Life), "Building a Community of Advocates," YouTube, September 24, 2021, educational video, https://www.youtube.com/watch?v=kO905RK57Rw&t=18s.

[2] https://www.flowauto.com/Home/ThreeCs.

[3] https://www.flowauto.com/Home/Service.

HABIT 28

ESTABLISH A CULTURE OF FORGIVENESS

Our team members are quick to forgive those who have wronged us.

Then Peter came up and said to Him, "Lord, how many times shall my brother sin against me and I still forgive him? Up to seven times?" Jesus said to him, "I do not say to you, up to seven times, but up to seventy-seven times."

—Matthew 18:21-22

Forgive us our debts as we forgive our debtors.

—Matthew 6:12

In business, there are times when we must forgive people who have mistreated, betrayed, cheated, and/or stolen from us. Sometimes, that forgiveness may have several zeros on the end of it. Three-figure forgiveness. Six-figure forgiveness. You may have to forgive even larger debts, depending on the scope of your transactions. Either way, it's a horrible experience.

How do you respond in business when people—employees, suppliers, contractors, owners, board members, vendors, customers, etc.—make promises they either cannot or will not keep?

HAVE YOU BEEN MISTREATED, BETRAYED, CHEATED, AND/OR ROBBED IN BUSINESS?

In a rush to get a fancy e-commerce website built for my new health and fitness services startup back in 2011, I hired an unqualified web developer (Mistake #1) and paid him in advance (Mistake #2). For the level of programming work I needed (or, thought I needed), I received several quotes from reputable web developers in the range of $25,000 USD to build the initial website. Considering I was a low-income business school student at the time, this far exceeded my budget. Plus, I only needed a functional prototype to get some initial users and demonstrate for investors.

In my search for a less-expensive option, I was referred to a web developer who had a website like the one I needed. His site was built for a different industry than mine, but it had the basic functionality. He promised he could duplicate his website and retrofit it to the specifications I needed for a $5,000 "licensing fee." Naïvely and impetuously, I paid the money.

I soon discovered he didn't actually have the skills to build what I needed, nor would he outsource the work to someone who was qualified. I waited for my website for six months, hoping this person would deliver on what he had promised. Once he confessed to me he would not deliver what he had promised, he promptly quit responding to my requests for a refund.

I had never before, nor since, felt such intense anger toward a colleague in business. At the time, I was soon-to-be-married and should have been focusing that squandered emotional energy on enjoying my season of engagement. Yet my anger toward the person who stole my money was robbing me of my joy. Emotionally, it was a torturous experience.

UNFORGIVENESS IS SELF-INFLICTED TORTURE.

Perhaps dealing with a client's breach of contract with his fishing company, Peter once asked Jesus,

"Lord, how often should I forgive someone who sins against me? Seven times?"

"No, not seven times," Jesus replied, "but seventy times seven!" (Matt. 18:21-22)

Jesus then told a sobering story from the business world about a man who had been forgiven a financial debt he could not pay. Despite the mercy shown toward him by his creditor, this man then turned around and refused to forgive a much smaller debt owed to him. Jesus said,

> The other servant fell on his knees and begged him, "Be patient with me, and I will pay you everything I owe."
>
> But the first servant refused to be patient. He threw the other servant into prison until he could pay everything he owed. When the other servants saw what had happened, they were very sorry. So they went and told their master all that had happened.
>
> Then the master called his servant in and said, "You evil servant! Because you begged me to forget what you owed, I told you that you did not have to pay anything. You should have showed mercy to that other servant, just as I showed mercy to you." The master was very angry and put the servant in prison to be punished until he could pay everything he owed.
>
> This king did what my heavenly Father will do to you if you do not forgive your brother or sister from your heart. (Matt. 18:29-35)

Based on this parable, are we to conclude that God will allow us to be tortured somehow if we refuse to forgive someone we believe has wronged us? Yes. Because God has offered to forgive us of so much more. That's why Jesus taught us to pray, "Forgive us our debts as we forgive our debtors" (Matt. 6:12). Unless we forgive others, God will not forgive us.

FORGIVENESS CLARIFIES OUR THINKING.

When we're living with unforgiveness, we are not in our right mind. It distorts our thinking and causes us to make foolish decisions.

As I began to reflect more deeply on how mercifully God has forgiven me for the sins I have committed, forgiving the person who stole $5,000 from me became much easier. Rather than spending more money, time, and energy to pursue legal action, I just forgave him. The emotional torture I was experiencing—a taste of the "torture" Jesus promised for those who refuse to forgive their debtors—simply was not worth $5,000.

As is often the case with scenarios like this one, that negative experience turned out to be a blessing in disguise. When the web development plan crumbled for my health and fitness startup, I decided to learn how to build the website myself. As I learned how to build a basic website, I quickly discovered I wasn't as passionate about that startup concept as I originally thought. I promptly applied my newly acquired skills toward building two websites for the purpose of promoting the ideas of Christian authors.

My act of forgiveness gave me the clarity of vision I needed to start and grow the successful publishing company I have been blessed with over the past nine years.

IF YOU'VE FORGIVEN SOMEONE, ACT LIKE IT.

Once you've truly forgiven someone, the Holy Spirit *may* lead you to take any of the following actions as expressions of that forgiveness:

- Pray for that person you've forgiven.
- Make it clear through your words and actions to anyone else directly involved in the conflict that you have indeed forgiven the person.
- Cease any legal actions you are taking against the person.
- Request that the person meet with you and a Christian mediator or arbitrator to finalize any details regarding the dispute.
- Refuse to gossip about the person.

Become a Better Steward ... Not a Better Doormat.

Now, you might be thinking, *The Bible also says, "An eye for an eye ... and a tooth for a tooth!" You can't be a doormat in the business world!* (We address this issue more in Habits 10, 18, 29, and 30, but it needs to be addressed here as well.) Good stewardship will help to minimize the number of times the decision to forgive in business will be forced upon you. Let me explain.

In addition to my experience of having $5,000 stolen from me, there have been a handful of other times when I was swindled in business (e.g., clients failing to pay, etc.). As I look back on these experiences, it was often my own poor stewardship that made me vulnerable to suffering such losses. In almost every case, my contract was not clear, I didn't do enough due diligence before making the decision, or there were no contingencies in place in the event that the agreement was breached.

Reflect on times when you have been mistreated, betrayed, cheated, and/or robbed in business. Write down ways you can become a better steward in those areas, such as ...

- Asking for the Holy Spirit's discernment
- Adding a new clause/contingency into your contracts
- Over-communicating and being consistent with your payment policies
- Seeking wise counsel
- Waiting an extra 24 hours before making a decision
- Getting detail-oriented people to help with your due diligence

At the same time, offenses will come, and we must learn to forgive others in business as God has forgiven us of debts we could never repay (Matt. 6:12).

REFLECTION, DISCUSSION, AND APPLICATION

How has God forgiven you?

What debts in business (e.g., mistreatments, betrayals, thefts, etc.) do you need to forgive?

As you have forgiven people in business, how has that fresh perspective and freedom affected your thinking, decisions, and behavior?

Habit 29

Use a Biblical Legal Process

If/when legal disputes are encountered and cannot be resolved between the opposing parties, we hire a reliable Christian mediator and/or arbitrator to assist in resolving the matter.

So if you have law courts dealing with matters of this life, do you appoint them as judges who are of no account in the church?

—1 Corinthians 6:4

Now if your brother sins, go and show him his fault in private; if he listens to you, you have gained your brother. But if he does not listen to you, take one or two more with you, so that on the testimony of two or three witnesses every matter may be confirmed. And if he refuses to listen to them, tell it to the church; and if he refuses to listen even to the church, he is to be to you as a Gentile and a tax collector.

—Matthew 18:15-17

*Now all these things are from God, who reconciled us to Himself
through Christ and gave us the ministry of reconciliation.*

—2 Corinthians 5:18

When Paul instructed first-century Christians in Corinth to avoid taking their legal cases to secular courts, he was writing at a time when it would have been nearly impossible to find a Christian judge. After all, the gospel had only recently landed in the Gentile world. This problem seems to be one of Paul's main reasons for instructing Christians to avoid taking their legal conflicts to secular courts.

Thankfully, due to the spread of the gospel over the past 2,000 years, there are many godly, Christian judges in today's courts in many countries around the world. Because of this blessing, most of us don't have to be as concerned that our case would be judged by a godless unbeliever if we decided to bring it to a government court. However, this doesn't mean we should bring our conflicts before government courts simply because many of the judges are Christians.

Paul says one problem with secular courts is that the judges are "of no account in the church" (1 Cor. 6:4). Even Christian judges—and nearly every other type of Christian professional—are rarely held to account by Christian Church leaders for the manner in which they live and conduct themselves in their professions.

Moreover, in most cases, a government would generally fire a judge who was thought to be held accountable to Church government or who publicly invoked God's counsel concerning a ruling on a case. This would likely be expedited by backlash from the liberal mainstream media. Christian judges are held to account by the government who employs them—rarely to the Church.

DO WE HAVE ALTERNATIVES TO GOVERNMENT-EMPLOYED JUDGES?

Why does Paul single out judges when almost no Christians of any profession are held to account by Christian Church leaders for their personal and professional conduct?

What if he had said, "Don't let a doctor give you medical advice unless she is held to account by the Christian Church?"

What if Paul said, "Don't do business with companies whose executives are not held to account by the Christian Church?" Even most Christian-owned businesses wouldn't be getting many Christian customers if believers lived by that standard.

What is so unique about a judge's role that Paul singled them out, implying Christians should not have their cases tried in their courts unless the judge is held to account by the Church?

Judges are responsible for hearing allegations of the prosecuting and defending parties, listening to witness testimony, and ruling on the admissibility of evidence. Paul suggests these services are available to people outside of government-owned-and-operated courts. Certainly, a judge employed by the government will rule on criminal cases in most societies, whether we like it or not. But we have far more options for mediation and arbitration when we have a civil case in need of a ruling. As such, Paul's admonition seems to refer specifically to these types of civil cases—usually involving money and business—for which we can choose whether a government judge will decide the case or if the conflict will be resolved in a different, more Christ-centered way.

For Paul, a judge is not limited to someone who went to law school, wears a black robe, and holds a gavel. As a Jewish lawyer himself (i.e., a Pharisee), Paul was especially keen to point out that a Greco-Roman judge in the 1st century would be woefully inadequate for rendering righteous legal decisions based on the full counsel of God, decisions that a Christ-following legal expert not employed by the government would be better equipped to make. To be sure, these Christ-following legal experts would need to be accountable to Church leaders on some level.

If your conflict has reached an impasse where you and the other party are unable to make peace without intervention from a third party, you might be thinking, *Who can I turn to who is a Christ-following legal expert accountable to Church leaders who will make a righteous decision concerning my legal dispute with a fellow business professional?*

CHRISTIAN MEDIATION

It could be that heightened negative emotions and unwillingness to communicate reasonably on either side of the disagreement has made it difficult for both sides to understand all the facts clearly regarding the dispute. A Christian mediator's job isn't to pass judgement in favor of one side or the other. The mediator's job is simply to bring both parties to the table and facilitate a conversation that will ideally resolve the conflict.

In some cases, the witness and accountability provided by a wise Christian mediator is enough to get two reasonable people to set aside their negative emotions and childish behavior to agree on peaceful terms.

CHRISTIAN ARBITRATION

A Christian arbitrator's job is, after hearing the facts of a dispute, to make a legally binding decision in favor of one party or the other, which is referred to as the *award*. Arbitration is similar to going to court but occurs in the private sector rather than in a government court. The major difference is that the two parties in the dispute get to decide who the judge will be — ideally, a wise and experienced Christian legal expert.

HOW CAN YOU ENCOURAGE THE OTHER PARTY TO AVOID TAKING THE CASE TO COURT?

You legally will not be able to prohibit your employees, customers, etc. from suing you and your company in court, but there are measures you can and should take to ensure a more Christ-centered legal process is attempted before resorting to government courts.

For example, consider including a conciliation statement like this one — written by *The Peacemaker* author, Ken Sande, and adopted by the Association of Christian Conciliation Services — in your contracts with new employees, clients, and other stakeholders:

The parties acknowledge that a conciliation process necessarily requires time and financial resources. To facilitate this process, [Your Company's Name] agrees to pay all initial fees and expenses that may be required by the mediator, case administrator, and/or arbitrator to carry out a conciliation process. The final apportionment between the parties of those fees and expenses shall be negotiated during mediation or, if necessary, decided by the arbitrator. The parties agree that they will make every reasonable effort to contain expenses by limiting the amount of fact-finding, investigation, and discovery to what is reasonably necessary to conduct a fair conciliation process.[1]

IS IT EVER RIGHT TO SUE?

Biblically speaking, is suing someone in a government court ever the right thing to do? If you can't get the accused party to meet you at the table with a Christian mediator or Christian arbitrator, these are about the only options you have remaining: 1) let the other party get away with whatever you're accusing them of having done or 2) sue the other party in court.

Aside from not getting the recompense due to you, if you just let them get away with whatever you believe they've done, it's more likely they'll keep doing it to others in the future. You may have a God-given responsibility to bring them before a judge, at least to help them think twice before trying to do something unlawful toward another business colleague in the future.

In any case, if/when legal disputes are encountered and cannot be resolved between the opposing parties, consider hiring a reliable Christian mediator and/or arbitrator who is accountable to the Church to assist in resolving the matter.

REFLECTION, DISCUSSION, AND APPLICATION

Do you include a Christian conciliation clause in your contracts? If not, do you plan to add one?

Who would you turn to for Christian mediation and/or arbitration if an unresolvable business dispute arose between you and a fellow Christian believer?

[1] This Conciliation Clause was written by Ken Sande and adopted by the Association of Christian Conciliation Services in 1990, with the understanding that they would be available to "any Christian conciliation ministry, church or other organization or person who wishes to encourage parties to resolve conflicts through Christian conciliation." Ownership of this material passed to the Institute for Christian Conciliation (ICC) in 1993. This material is published through RW360 pursuant to a special license from the ICC. https://rw360.org/conciliation-clauses/.

PART SIX

RISK MANAGEMENT

Follow this QR code to take the
Christ-Centered Company Assessment.

HABIT 30

ASSESS YOUR RISK

Our company has conducted a thorough assessment of our company's risk exposure.

The prudent see danger and take refuge, but the simple keep going and pay the penalty.

—Proverbs 27:12, NIV

Behold, I am sending you out as sheep in the midst of wolves; so be as wary as serpents, and as innocent as doves.

—Matthew 10:16

Jesus recognizes that there's risk in what we do in service to him in the marketplace. Most of us encounter "wolves" in business daily. There are threats to our livelihoods and companies on all sides. Here are some of the "wolves" hunting for you and your company that could result in lawsuits, major unforeseen expenses, troubles with the government, damages to your company's reputation, and more:

- Hacking, ransomware, and other cybersecurity threats
- Natural disasters, pandemics, economic, and geopolitical crises

- Shoplifting and employee theft
- Negative ratings and reviews posted about your company in public forums
- Uncertainties and errors related to governmental regulations and tax codes
- Adopting wrong technologies
- Costly employee errors
- Errors and omissions on behalf of a client
- Lawsuits from disgruntled employees

Solomon said, "the prudent see danger and take refuge, but the simple keep going and pay the penalty" (Prov. 27:12, NIV). To prevent the marketplace wolves from devouring you and your business, you must plan effectively.

Yes, we should have a clear sense of purpose, values, goals, and marketing strategy as discussed in "Part 1" and "Part 2" of this book. At the same time, as General George Patton said, "No plan ever survived contact with the enemy." In addition to deliberate planning based on a set of assumptions, you will also need a disaster response plan to implement when things go wrong.

SHREWD PLANNING

As marketplace Christians, we have a sacred obligation to manage well the resources God has entrusted to us. But why did Jesus tell us to be "shrewd as serpents?" (Matt. 10:16) That almost sounds like Jesus is exhorting us to be deceitful in business. What does it mean to be "shrewd as serpents?"

The word translated as *shrewd* means "acting with or showing care or thought for the future." The master in Jesus' Parable of the Shrewd Manager said the manager demonstrated this kind of shrewdness when he, immediately after his master fired him, marked down the debts of those indebted to his master. In doing so, the manager banked a tremendous amount of goodwill with his master's debtors. His master commended him because he was planning for his own future.

Jesus also emphasized the importance of shrewd planning for the future in the Parable of the Tower Builder:

For which one of you, when he wants to build a tower, does not first sit down and calculate the cost to see if he has enough to complete it? (Luke 14:28)

This verse has been interpreted as an admonition to factor in foreseen costs associated with a particular endeavor (e.g., in this case, the endeavor of being a follower of Jesus). Certainly, a builder should consider unforeseen costs as well. Let's explore some practical ways to do this.

GET THE RIGHT INSURANCE COVERAGE.

Have you purchased the insurance you and your company need? Here are some examples of common insurances purchased by Christ-centered companies:

- **General liability insurance** – Protects your company from claims that it caused bodily injuries and property damage.
- **Property insurance** – Protects buildings and property you own (i.e., offices, equipment, and tools) that your company needs to perform essential functions.
- **Errors and omissions insurance** – Protects your company from lawsuits claiming your company made a mistake in your professional services that cost your client extra money.
- **Cybersecurity insurance** – Reduces financial risks associated with doing business online.
- **Key man insurance** (i.e., business life insurance policy) – Protects against financial loss if an owner, partner, top executive, or essential employee passes away.
- **Workers compensation insurance** – Protects your company and your workforce by providing benefits to most employees injured on the job.
- **Business income insurance** – Protects against loss of business income if you can't operate because of a covered peril.

DEVELOP AND MAINTAIN A DISASTER RECOVERY PLAN.

Texas Injection Molding maintains a disaster recovery plan in the event that a major disaster (e.g., natural disaster, public health crisis, etc.) temporarily shuts down their operations. In addition to providing guidance regarding filing insurance claims, etc., the plan includes guidance on which industry peers they will rely on to service their customers until they are able to resume operations.

KNOW WHO TO CALL BEFORE DISASTER STRIKES.

If your company was sued today, who would you call for legal representation? If someone got hurt physically or financially as a result of doing business with you, would you and your company be at risk if you got sued?

Who would you call for help if you were just notified that the IRS is planning to audit your company?

Make sure you know who to call before the "wolves" attack. If you're not ready and protected, one lawsuit, audit, or major unforeseen crisis could shut down your business. Be shrewd and take the necessary time to identify every area of your company vulnerable to these threats. As an Air Force logistician, one of our unofficial "loggie" slogans was this: "Plan for the worst. Hope for the best." When it comes to your company's risk management, that's a philosophy worth adopting.

REFLECTION, DISCUSSION, AND APPLICATION

What are the areas of your business where you are exposed to varying degrees of risk?

What insurance policies do you need? Do you already have them in place?

What is your company's disaster response plan?

HABIT 31

GUARD YOUR REPUTATION

Our company is proactive about guarding our company's reputation.

A good name is to be more desired than great wealth; favor is better than silver and gold.

—Proverbs 22:1

If you ask most people for an example of a "Christ-centered company," Chick-fil-A will typically be the first one named. This is primarily because protecting its "good name" (based on Proverbs 22:1) was one of Chick-fil-A founder Truett Cathy's guiding biblical principles in establishing the company. From its God-oriented purpose statement to its relentless commitment to going the "extra mile" for its customers and employees, the enduring "good name" legacy of Truett Cathy through Chick-fil-A was built by design.

In business, our greatest and most lasting achievement will be that the company cultures we're building lead people closer to Jesus. This is the Christ-centered "good name" we are called to cultivate and protect as individuals and company influencers. Following the examples of Truett Cathy and countless other Christ-centered company leaders, be proactive about guarding your company's "good name" to ensure your company's culture and habits are leading people toward Jesus.

DID JESUS DEFEND HIS "GOOD NAME"?

How did Jesus react when people said false things about him? If we haven't studied his behavior as recorded in the four Gospels, we might assume his response was always to "turn the other cheek" as he instructed his disciples to do. For Jesus, did "turn the other cheek" mean we ought to say nothing when people speak lies against us publicly or even privately? Certainly not!

"Turn the other cheek" was Jesus' admonition to avoid taking revenge; it was not a mandate to be a doormat and let people spread lies about you and your company without rebuking them. People frequently said and implied things about Jesus that were false. And Jesus didn't let them get away with it by saying nothing. Here are a few examples:

- **Criticism from John the Baptist**: "When John the Baptist was in prison, he heard what Jesus was doing. He sent his followers. They asked, 'Are You the One Who was to come, or should we look for another?'"(Matt. 11:2-3)

  o **Jesus' retort**: "Jesus said to them, 'Go and tell John what you see and hear. The blind are made to see. Those who could not walk are walking. Those who have had bad skin diseases are healed. Those who could not hear are hearing. The dead are raised up to life and the Good News is preached to poor people. He is happy who is not ashamed of Me and does not turn away because of Me.'" (Matt. 11:4-6)

- **Criticism from the Pharisees**: "The Son of Man came eating and drinking, and they say, 'Behold, a gluttonous man and a heavy drinker, a friend of tax collectors and sinners!'" (Matt. 11:19a)

  o **Jesus' retort**: "And yet wisdom is vindicated by her deeds."(Matt. 11:19b)

- **Criticism from the scribes**: "And the scribes who came down from Jerusalem said, "He is possessed by Beelzebub, and by the ruler of the demons He casts out demons." (Mark 3:22)

  o **Jesus' retort**: "So He called them to Him and said to them in parables, 'How can Satan cast out Satan?

If a kingdom is divided against itself, that kingdom cannot stand. If a house is divided against itself, that house cannot stand. And if Satan rises up against himself and is divided, he cannot stand, but is coming to an end. No one can enter a strong man's house and plunder his goods, unless he first binds the strong man. Then he will plunder his house.'" (Mark 3:23-27)

In each of these examples, Jesus didn't simply respond by clarifying his intentions or motives. Instead, he redirected the accuser's attention back to the integrity of his ministry and the results he had produced. He was confident enough to allow his performance to stand on its own merits.

Paul writes that Jesus "made of himself no reputation" (Phil. 2:7), but this doesn't mean Jesus didn't control the narrative about his identity. As I point out in *Marketing Like Jesus*, he used many descriptive metaphors and claims to brand himself in the minds of people: "bread of life" (John 6:48), "the way, the truth, and the life" (John 14:6), "the good shepherd" (John 10:11), "the true vine" (John 15:1), and more.

He inquired what people thought about him, especially wanting to know what his closest disciples thought about him. He asked them,

- "Who do people say that the Son of Man is?" (Matt. 16:13)
- "But who do you yourselves say that I am?" (Matt. 16:15)

Certainly, he knew them and their thoughts better than they knew themselves, but he still asked for their feedback with the goal of helping them to become better disciples.

What are some practical ways we can monitor our company's reputation over time to find out what people are thinking and saying about us, giving us opportunities to respond appropriately? This knowledge will help us to cultivate and protect our company's "good name."

ASK FOR CUSTOMER FEEDBACK IN PRIVATE.

Whether their negative criticism is valid or not, it's always better to have your customers share any negative feedback about your company privately rather than finding out about it in a public forum where the damage to your company's reputation will be more significant. Asking for their feedback in private also helps to build trust and mutual respect with your customers as this approach communicates that their perspectives truly matter to you.

A simple and effective tool for requesting and monitoring this type of feedback is a *net promoter score* (NPS). Ask your customers this question at regular intervals: "On a scale of 1-10, how likely are you to recommend us to a friend or colleague?" The current average of your customers' responses to this question is your net promoter score (NPS) at any given time. Here's a quick guide to interpreting each person's NPS response:

- 9-10 = **Promoters** (These people are extremely likely to recommend your company to others.)

- 7-8 = **Passives** (These people are somewhat indifferent toward your company.)

- 1-6 = **Detractors** (These people are not likely to recommend you to others and may be actively encouraging people to avoid your company.)

As you ask your customers to rate your company on a scale of 1-10, be sure to give them an option to leave any comments about why they rated you as such.

MONITOR WHAT PEOPLE ARE SAYING ABOUT YOUR COMPANY PUBLICLY.

Conduct a Google search for your company's name and take an inventory of where and how your company is being mentioned on the internet. Here are some of the most influential public forums shaping people's perceptions of today's companies, products, and services:

- For companies selling products online: Amazon product ratings/reviews

- For companies selling services and products locally: Google ratings/reviews

- Companies seeking to attract top talent: Glassdoor.com
- Small businesses seeking referrals from other small businesses: Alignable.com

As you are assessing your company's reputation on the internet, ensure you're not excessively checking your ratings, reviews, and mentions for the purpose of ego gratification. This habit cuts both ways as an obsession with the volatile opinions of others could cause you and your company to follow public perceptions rather than the leadership of the Holy Spirit.

APPROACH CUSTOMER COMPLAINTS WITH GENTLENESS AND EAGERNESS TO IMPROVE WHERE NECESSARY.

You, your family, and your team could spend decades building goodwill with your stakeholders—making sacrifices of time, opportunities, money, and more—only to have someone seek to damage your reputation on the internet without making a good-faith effort to resolve the conflict privately and peacefully. Such a detractor couldn't care less because he likely has no idea what it takes to build a company. When such people get offended, they turn vindictive and will stop at nothing to cause as much damage to your company's reputation as possible.

Nevertheless, other customers have legitimate complaints that can be assets to your company if you will allow them to be. Be sure to respond to these complaints quickly. Don't just view them as inconveniences. These are some of your greatest opportunities to represent the character of Jesus to those who do business with your company. If you will invite and remain open to negative criticism from your customers, you will recognize that the criticism is accompanied by one or more of the following opportunities:

- To present humble, Christ-like character with responses to the customer bathed in the spiritual fruit of gentleness
- To make your agreements more clear

- To compensate a customer for unfulfilled promises you've made to her
- To add another helpful service/product or a helpful feature to an existing service/product

When viewed redemptively, negative criticism from your customers (and team members) can be one of your greatest assets.

REQUEST PUBLIC REVIEWS FROM HAPPY CUSTOMERS.

Proverbs doesn't say, "A name *that doesn't have any negative public criticism* is worth more than gold." It says, "*A good name* is worth more than gold." We want a good name, not merely one free and clear of any negative criticism. Our aim regarding the protection of our company's reputation isn't merely to do damage control of negative reviews. Our focus ought to be on ensuring that positive customer feedback is so abundant and ubiquitous that it drowns out the voices of the detractors in the minds of people considering doing business with our companies.

Encourage your happy and satisfied customers to leave reviews for your company, its products, and its services publicly to build the social proof necessary to show the world your company has a "good name." Typically, all you must do is ask them to post a public review and provide some basic instructions on where and how to post the review.

REFLECTION, DISCUSSION, AND APPLICATION

Does your company have a "good name?" How do you know?

What results have you produced for your customers? (see Habit 8)

How do you request customer feedback?

How do you respond if/when somebody says or posts something negative about your company in a public forum?

Where is the ideal place where you'd want happy customers to leave public reviews about your company?

HABIT 32

DIVERSIFY

Our company has a diversified product/service offering and a commitment to innovate so we can succeed in changing environments.

Divide your portion to seven, or even to eight, for you do not know what misfortune may occur on the earth.

—Ecclesiastes 11:2

This expression, "Yet once more," denotes the removing of those things which can be shaken, as of created things, so that those things which cannot be shaken may remain.

—Hebrews 12:27

The COVID-19 lockdowns devastated thousands of companies, especially those that didn't have diversified product and service offerings. For example, thousands of restaurants that weren't ready to promote online ordering, carry-out, and food delivery services aggressively were soon shuttered once eating inside restaurants was outlawed due to social-distancing restrictions.

Thousands more brick-and-mortar retail stores without an ecommerce presence saw their sales plummet, having no other means to generate revenue. Some scrambled to get their products listed for sale online, but for many, it was too late.

Perhaps some of those companies would have remained in business through the pandemic if they would have heeded this biblical wisdom: "Divide your portion to seven, or even to eight, for you do not know what misfortune may occur on the earth" (Ecc. 11:2).

WHAT "DISASTERS" COULD COME UPON YOUR COMPANY?

Disasters will come. The Bible says, "This expression, 'Yet once more,' denotes the removing of those things which can be shaken, as of created things, so that those things which cannot be shaken may remain" (Heb. 12:27). Besides a global pandemic, the following circumstances could present a disaster scenario, a "shaking" for your company:

- Disruptive technology directly affecting your company/industry
- War in a region where your company operates
- Cybersecurity breach
- One of your team members being involved in a scandal
- Labor shortages
- Natural disaster damaging your assets and/or supply chain
- Geopolitical problems damaging the supply chain for your products

Diversification is one critical means of managing these risks to the company God has entrusted to you.

DIVERSIFY WITH UNTAPPED OR UNDER-TAPPED PROFIT CENTERS CURRENTLY IN YOUR COMPANY.

When supply chain shortages for pocket doors (i.e., doors that slide and hide within the wall) made it difficult for retailer McCoy Building Supply to make these products available to their customers, they decided to turn their problem into a solution. They began manufacturing pocket doors in-house, providing their company with yet another strong profit center.

Before launching new products, services, value propositions, and brands, fully leverage the potential of areas in your business that could be producing more if you started investing more of your attention and resources into them.

DIVERSIFY WITH NEW TECHNOLOGY.

My company operates in the publishing industry, which has been transformed over the past 20 years through innovations such as digital print on-demand, ecommerce, ebooks, digital audiobooks, and more. While large brick-and-mortar bookstores are dying, printed books are still in high demand. But readers also prefer to learn from authors through a wide range of other media such as ebooks, audiobooks, podcast episodes, video courses, webinars, blog articles, and social media posts. We must stay in tune and adapt as necessary with the shifts occurring in our industry. We won't stop printing books anytime soon, but we will diversify our value propositions by leveraging new publishing technologies.

What technologies have emerged in your market that you should at least have your team start experimenting with to assess their potential benefits for your company?

Now is the time to diversify your company's assets and revenue sources. Don't wait for the next disaster to come upon the land before you and your team start taking the necessary actions to diversify.

REFLECTION, DISCUSSION, AND APPLICATION

What are the most likely disasters that could negatively impact your company?

How could your company become more diversified as a hedge against potential disasters that may impact your company in the future?

HABIT 33

AVOID DEBT

Our company maintains a conservative debt-to-equity ratio.

The rich rules over the poor, and the borrower becomes the lender's slave.

—Proverbs 22:7

For the Lord your God will have blessed you just as He has promised you, and you will lend to many nations, but you will not borrow; and you will rule over many nations, but they will not rule over you.

—Deuteronomy 15:6

You shall not covet your neighbor's house; you shall not covet your neighbor's wife, or his male servant, or his female servant, or his ox, or his donkey, or anything that is your neighbor's.

—Exodus 20:17

Jacto Agricultural Machines—which is currently present in 100 countries and has factories in Brazil, Argentina, and Thailand—was so deeply in debt in the 1970s that two-thirds of its profits were needed just to pay the

THE CHRIST-CENTERED COMPANY

interest on their loans. The company's leaders decided to make the company permanently debt-free in 1981 and accomplished that goal within two years. The company's Christian founder, Shunji Nishimura, said,

> In 2007, we decided to keep at least two-month's revenue in cash as capital reserves. Today, the company has enough in strategic cash reserves to service the company's expenses for 12 months with no revenue. Being debt-free with significant cash reserves enables us to determine our destiny and continue to improve—no matter what ... There have been a couple of times during economic crisis in Brazil that we have earned more on the interest of our capital reserves than the company earned before the crisis![1]

The Bible says, "The rich rules over the poor, and the borrower becomes the lender's slave" (Prov. 22:7). An employee can quit working for an employer at any time, but a slave is bound to the master until the debt is paid in full. If a business owner takes out a five-year loan, she—and, by extension, the company she owns—has become a five-year servant of the bank.

The prophet Habbakuk said,

> Woe to him who increases what is not his—for how long—and makes himself rich with loans? Will not your creditors rise up suddenly, and those who collect from you awaken? Indeed, you will become plunder for them. (Hab. 2:6-7)

Don't allow yourself and your company to "increase what is not [yours]" by becoming "rich with loans." Solomon said that such a person "pretends to be rich, but has nothing" (Prov. 13:7). Borrowing money may artificially reduce stress in the short term, giving you extra cash flow so you can spend that borrowed money on some aspect of your business. But allowing your company to become a slave to lenders, which ties up your cash flow, will inhibit your ability to seize opportunities to grow organically. Don't use debt as a bailout or growth-booster. Focus on how to reduce your expenses and, more importantly, how to increase revenue.

While there are some wise reasons for a company and its owners to borrow money, there are typically two things that drive business owners to get loans: 1) mismanagement and 2) coveting. Guard your company against both traps.

DON'T GET A LOAN TO FIX MISMANAGEMENT.

If there is ever a good time to borrow money, it's certainly not when your company is struggling because of mismanagement. Yet that is often when taking out loans feels most necessary. It's like throwing gas on a fire with the goal of quenching it. That gas will simply magnify the problem.

Borrowing money seems like an easier, more convenient way to keep the business going in the short term. And if all you care about is the short term, go get that loan. There are plenty of small business lenders who would love to become your creditors. You probably get their solicitations through the mail, email, and text messaging daily.

But if you're more interested in the long-term health of your company, don't borrow money when you're struggling. Make the difficult decisions to cut your costs, no matter how painful. And figure out how to squeeze more revenue out of untapped and under-tapped areas of your business.

DON'T GET A LOAN BECAUSE YOU'RE COVETING WHAT YOU DON'T HAVE.

Do you ever catch yourself being jealous of the size of another company? Did you then conclude the reason your peer's company is bigger than yours is because you have been deprived of the financial capital he or she somehow acquired?

The Bible labels this type of thinking and behavior as *coveting*, and the Tenth Commandment is, "You shall not covet."

The next thought in this destructive cycle of coveting in business is often this: *We need to borrow some money and get bigger!*

When business leaders covet, destructive consequences always follow for the companies they lead. Often, that coveting puts both the company and the company's leader into the financial bondage of indebtedness as the leader seeks to keep up with his peers or some other standard outside of God's will. Revisit "Habit 6: Focus More on Getting Better Than Bigger" if you and your company are stuck in the trap of comparing the size of your company to others'.

BE CONTENT.

As we focus on being content, grateful, and responsible with what God has entrusted to us, we won't feel compelled to purchase things we and our companies cannot afford and that aren't consistent with our purpose, values, and goals. Paul writes, "Godliness with contentment is great gain" (1 Tim. 6:6). It is impossible to honor God with what we have if we aren't grateful for what we have. Paul said,

> I am not saying this because I am in need, for I have learned to be content whatever the circumstances. I know what it is to be in need, and I know what it is to have plenty. I have learned the secret of being content in any and every situation, whether well fed or hungry, whether living in plenty or in want. (Phil. 4:11-12)

Contentment helps us focus on delayed gratification so we won't gratify every impulsive desire. Gratitude enhances our ability to expect greater financial increase and opportunities from God. Gratitude flows from the understanding that there is an abundance of wealth waiting to be created, overcoming the deception that we must borrow the wealth others have created to be successful.

GOD IS NOT NECESSARILY AGAINST LENDING MONEY.

Moses prophesied, "The Lord will make you abound in prosperity ... *you shall lend to many nations*, but *you shall not borrow*" (Deut. 28:11-12, emphasis mine). Because lending is a two-way exchange, God wouldn't suggest lending could be an ideal practice while simultaneously forbidding borrowing. God never outlawed borrowing money. Instead, the Bible makes it clear that borrowing simply isn't part of God's best plan for his people. At the same time, his intention is for his people to do the lending rather than the borrowing.

Does God want your company to borrow money?

While debt shouldn't be used as a bailout, debt could be used wisely to keep up with existing demand for your products and services, particularly when your vendors are slow to pay. I have had vendors delay payments for as long as an entire year, which is completely unacceptable yet something we can't completely control. Ideally, you'd be able to fund that inventory or payroll with cash flow to keep selling your products and services, but this isn't always an option.

If taking on debt is wise for your company, ensure your debt-to-equity ratio remains less than 0.5.

- 0 = Company does not finance expenses through debt at all.
- 0.5 = Twice as much equity as debt. Investors own two-thirds of the company's assets.
- 1 = Creditors and investors own equal parts of company assets.
- 1.5 = For every dollar in equity, the company owes $1.50 to creditors.
- 2 = Twice as much debt as equity. Creditors own two thirds of company assets.

As you factor in all the positive and negative consequences of borrowing money for your company, the most important factor is this: *What is God instructing you to do?*

Reflection, Discussion, and Application

What is your company's debt-to-equity ratio?

If you borrow money for your company, what is your justification for doing so?

---

[1] Jeff Holler, *Bigger Than Business* (Houston: High Bridge Books, 2018), 89.

PART SEVEN

PHILANTHROPY

Follow this QR code to take the
Christ-Centered Company Assessment.

Habit 34

Tithe and Give

As an influencer of my company, I demonstrate that God is the source of everything my company needs by tithing at least 10 percent of my personal income to the Lord.

Here mortal men receive tithes, but there He [Jesus] receives them, of whom it is witnessed that He lives.

—Hebrews 7:8

Do you generally feel stuck in a trap of small thinking, unable to see your company through the lens of God's limitless resources? Do you lack a massive vision for your life and the company you influence?

If so, I know of something that might help. It's called *tithing*, the biblical habit of returning the first 10 percent of your income to God, which can be done by giving toward the following types of endeavors:

1. Individuals and/or organizations who are discipling you and your own family as followers of Jesus

2. Efforts that help to disciple other people as followers of Jesus

3. Meeting financial needs of the poor

4. Meeting financial needs of your lower-income employees when they have a financial challenge their wages are insufficient to meet

If a business owner is not tithing at least 10 percent toward these types of Christ-centered endeavors, both his personal finances and those of his company are being robbed of God's blessing and perspective.

You've probably heard the story of when Abram tithed in Genesis. Do you realize what happened immediately *after* he tithed? Let's start with a recap.

TITHING IDENTIFIES WHO YOU VIEW AS YOUR SOURCE.

After experiencing victory on the battlefield during the war against the kings of Sodom and Gomorrah, Abram felt compelled by love and gratitude to honor God by returning the first 10 percent of the spoils to God, the one he viewed as the source of his victory. He did this by returning the tithe to God through Melchizedek, "a priest of God Most High" (Gen. 14:17-20). The New Testament explains this process as follows:

> Here mortal men receive tithes, but there He [Jesus] receives them, of whom it is witnessed that He lives. (Heb. 7:8)

In other words, when we tithe, Jesus is on the receiving end.

After tithing to God through Melchizedek, Abram's loyalty to God was immediately tested.

> The king of Sodom said to Abram, "Give the people to me and take the goods for yourself."
>
> Abram said to the king of Sodom, "I have sworn to the Lord God Most High, possessor of heaven and earth, that I will not take a thread or sandal thong or anything that is yours, for fear you would say, 'I have made Abram rich.'" (Gen. 14:21)

Abram viewed God as his source—not himself and certainly not some wicked king.

Not only does tithing test our love and loyalty to God, it tests whether we consider God as our source. Having tithed to God, Abram's loyalty was confirmed, despite the invitation to put riches before God and others.

If you are your own source, keep the tithe. But if God is your source, return the tithe to Him. Just be advised that he is a much more reliable source for what you and your company need.

TITHING CAN OPEN YOUR EYES TO A MASSIVE VISION.

What happened immediately after Abram tithed reveals a powerful by-product of tithing: a massive vision.

> After these things [the account of Abram's tithe to Melchize-dek] the word of the Lord came to Abram in a vision, saying, "Do not fear, Abram, I am a shield to you; Your reward shall be very great ... Now look toward the heavens, and count the stars, if you are able to count them ... so shall your descendants be. Then he believed in the Lord; and He reckoned it to him as righteousness." (Gen. 15:1, 5-6)

If Abram would have accepted what the King of Sodom was offering in exchange for his loyalty to God, he would not have had the faith and vision to expect greater acts and revelations from God. Because Abram tithed, he was prepared to resist the temptation to credit anything but God as the source of his victory and provision. As a result, Abram's trust in God increased, opening his eyes to behold God's destiny for his life and for his people.

Tithing is not merely a financial issue. Tithing helps to prepare us for fulfilling the will of God in every aspect of our lives. It is a constant expression of our dependence upon God that enables us to believe him for greater things concerning our companies, relationships, health, finances, and more. Tithing prepares us to receive God's vision for our personal and professional lives. It is a habit of faith that helps us believe God for the impossible, not merely for what we can achieve through the unreliable source of our feeble human strength.

The Bible says, "All the tithe of the land ... is the Lord's" (Lev. 27:30). At no point in history has this reality become less of a reality. All tithes belong to the Lord. Period. That's because he is the source of all things.

"The earth is the Lord's, and all it contains, the world, and those who dwell in it" (Psa. 24:1).

Each time we receive a financial blessing, God eagerly observes to see if we will express our reliance on him by returning the first 10 percent of each paycheck, dividend, gift, inheritance, etc. to him. He wants to know if we will acknowledge him as our source or if we are hell-bent on viewing ourselves as our own counterfeit, woefully inadequate sources of provision.

YOU DON'T HAVE TO STOP AT 10 PERCENT.

When they founded Barnhart Crane and Rigging, brothers Alan and Eric Barnhart decided how much money would be enough for their families to live in reasonable comfort. They targeted that salary, committing to give away anything beyond that number. Of the remainder, 50 percent of profits went back into the business, and 50 percent went to Christian ministries. Alan and Eric gave away $50,000 during their first year of business, an amount that exceeded either of their salaries. Today, the company has now given away over $100 million toward Christian ministries.

R.G. LeTourneau "reverse tithed" the profits from his heavy machinery company, donating 90 percent to Christian causes and living on 10 percent.

Stanley Tam gave his charitable giving foundation 100 percent ownership of his company, U.S. Plastic Corporation.

Hobby Lobby donates 50 percent of its pre-tax profits to charitable causes. If Hobby Lobby were to be sold, 90 percent of the proceeds would go to its nonprofit foundation to be disbursed for ministry purposes. David Green, the founder of Hobby Lobby, tells his family and would likely tell any business leader, "God didn't put any of us here to sit on a yacht."[1]

Start by demonstrating that God is the source of everything your company needs by tithing at least 10 percent of your personal income to the Lord.

REFLECTION, DISCUSSION, AND APPLICATION

Do you tithe? If so, has tithing helped you to think bigger, knowing that God is your source for everything?

---

[1] David Green, *More Than a Hobby* (Nashville: Thomas Nelson, 2010), 195.

HABIT 35

GIVE IN SECRET

We keep our corporate charitable giving Christ-centered
rather than giving as a means of branding, advertising, or
public relations.

---

*But when you give to the poor, do not let your left hand know what
your right hand is doing.*

—Matthew 6:3

Tobacco giant Philip Morris spent $115 million on its charitable contri-
butions in the year 2000, while spending $150 million on an advertis-
ing campaign to publicize those donations. The recipients of that $115
million were probably able to do a lot of social good with that money, but
considering how much money they spent on telling the world where that
money came from, it seems those charitable contributions were primarily
about improving public perceptions of Philip Morris.[1]

Would you consider their $115 million donations as "charitable?" De-
spite the somewhat evident conflict of interest, the IRS tax code classified
their $115 million worth of donations as tax-deductible, charitable contri-
butions.

But, as usual, Jesus' standards are higher than the world's. He said,
"But when you give to the poor, do not let your left hand know what your
right hand is doing" (Matt. 6:3). In other words, when giving to honor the

Lord and bless others, do it without seeking praise for your good deed. In general, this means doing it in secret.

ADVERTISING AND A SOCIALLY CONSCIOUS THEMED BRAND DO NOT EQUATE TO TITHING OR CHRIST-CENTERED GIVING.

If you're going to spend money on advertising, that's potentially a good and noble thing, particularly if your company is adding value to people's lives in a Christ-centered way. But it's unwise to call it "charitable giving" if you're looking to get anything in exchange for it other than the private affirmation that comes only from the Lord.

If you make a "sponsorship" contribution on behalf of your company toward a nonprofit homeless shelter's fundraising banquet, for example, knowing you're going to get a reserved table at the front and your name in the program, you're letting your left hand know what your right hand is doing. But it's a great advertising opportunity for your company. And that's probably a good thing. It just doesn't equate to tithing or Christ-centered giving above the tithe.

If you suggest in your advertising and branding that people should do business with you because you're going to donate part of the sales revenue to a charity, you're letting your right hand know what your left hand is doing. But you may have a winning business model in today's socially conscious marketplace. And that's probably a good thing. It just doesn't equate to tithing or Christ-centered giving above the tithe.

Keep your corporate charitable giving Christ-centered rather than giving as a means of branding, advertising, or public relations.

REFLECTION, DISCUSSION, AND APPLICATION

Do you make a clear distinction between advertising/PR investments and charitable giving? Or do you tend to blur the lines?

---

[1] "Corporate Goodwill or Tainted Money?," February 8, 2001, ABC News, https://abcnews.go.com/WNT/story?id=131249&page=1.

TAKE CARE OF YOUR HOUSEHOLD FIRST

Our company ensures that the needs of our team members are addressed before giving profits away outside the company.

But if anyone does not provide for his own, and especially for those of his household, he has denied the faith and is worse than an unbeliever.

—1 Timothy 5:8

In the Bible, the term "household" encompasses more people than the nuclear family (i.e., dad, mom, and the kids). It includes all the people involved in the economic engine owned by the head-of-household.

When Abraham heard his nephew Lot had been captured, he summoned "318 trained men who had been born *in his household*" to go rescue him (Gen. 14:14, emphasis mine). That's a big household!

If Abraham wouldn't have had a son, the person who would have received his entire estate was a man named Eliezer of Damascus (Gen. 15:2). He was one of Abraham's employees and "the elder of his house, that ruled over all that he had" (Gen. 24:2). Imagine that. Had there been no biological heir, Abraham's inheritance would have been given to one of his employees.

The Bible says a righteous businesswoman named Lydia, "a seller of purple fabrics," got baptized as well as her entire household. This "household" consisted of the blood-related relatives who lived with her as well as the people employed within her company (Acts 16:14-15). When she got baptized, everyone in her household followed her example.

Biblically speaking, the people employed by the company you own are part of your household. Your team members probably don't live in the same house as you, but you bear significant responsibility for their livelihoods.

IS YOUR HOUSEHOLD TAKEN CARE OF FIRST?

Business leaders are, by and large, viewed as the ATM machines of the church and nonprofit world. It feels good to know that a few charitable organizations have at least some financial dependence on us to carry out their missions. They often invest into making this dynamic feel extra good through lavish fundraising banquets that target big donors, naming facilities after top donors, granting flattering titles such as "President's Club Donor," etc.

But this has a dark side, and that dark side has been yielded to when the needs of the people within one's own company are consistently unaccounted for and unmet.

Before you look toward giving charitably to needs outside of your company, first aim to meet the needs among your own team members. As a business leader, they are part of your household. Consider this verse:

> But if anyone does not provide for his own, and especially for those of his household, he has denied the faith and is worse than an unbeliever. (1 Tim. 5:8)

You might be tempted to think, *Well, I'm paying their wages, so that should be sufficient for meeting their needs.* Indeed, paying wages to someone is a noble deed. But that doesn't mean those wages are sufficient to cover needs like these, particularly for lower-paid team members:

- Funeral expenses for a loved one who passed away
- An expensive car repair
- An expensive home repair
- An expensive medical bill

After noticing one of his company's team members walking to work on a hot day, the owner of Demos' Restaurants, Peter Demos, distributed a survey to the company's employees to find out who didn't have viable transportation to get to work. In response to the survey, the company purchased 20 bikes for their employees, had the company's chaplains pray over them, and explained to their employees that the love of Jesus prompted the act of kindness.

Taking care of their household doesn't stop there. To help employees and their families who are struggling to have enough food, Demos' Restaurants now has a section of their menu with items that are free exclusively for employees. They also distribute food boxes to their team members' family members that include non-perishable food items.[1]

Chris Patton, current CEO of His Way at Work and President of Mike Patton Auto in LaGrange, Georgia, said,

> We were giving away about 90 percent of our charitable giving budget outside the company and only 10 percent inside. If I could go back to 2004, I would give away 10 percent outside and 90 percent inside the company.

SET UP A SUSTAINABLE CHARITABLE GIVING PROGRAM TO HELP EMPLOYEES IN NEED.

To take care of the employees in your household, you will need a sustainable system to help financially support employees facing occasional financial burdens they are unable to carry with their wages alone.

Perhaps the best model for charitable giving to employees in need has been developed by an organization called His Way at Work (HWAW). Their model developed within a large manufacturing company named Polydeck and has since been replicated successfully in companies worldwide.

In the HWAW model, if a team member has an occasional need like the ones listed in the section above (e.g., car repair, etc.), a collection will be taken up from among their fellow team members.

The employer will then match those contributions dollar for dollar from a special fund set up for the employee-run giving committee to manage. In this manner, the team members at all levels of the company, rather than the company's owner(s) and executives, decide which needs will receive the most (and least) amount of financial support. This model takes the pressure off the senior leaders and empowers the other team members.

Here are some steps to implement a program like this to take care of your "household" (i.e., company):

- Give your program a name. For example, it might be "[YOUR COMPANY NAME] Cares" (e.g., XYZ Services Cares).

- Set a monthly matching contribution amount. This is the maximum amount the company will pay out to employees' needs each month.

- Publish a basic application for employees to submit their requests for support. This could be a paper form or an online form (e.g., Google Forms).

- Appoint a committee of at least 1-3 employees to manage the program, which includes the following responsibilities:

  o Process team members' need applications

  o Steward the company's giving fund

  o Process financial contributions donated by employees

By default (in the U.S.), these gifts to employees will be considered by the IRS as taxable income to those employees. Here are a few ways employers can alleviate this burden:

- Some employers agree to pay their employees' income taxes (i.e., "gross up") for any/all gifts given through the employee giving fund.

- Some employers use a process through National Christian Foundation (NCF) that allows these gifts to be received tax-free. If interested, contact them at https://www.ncfgiving.com/contact/.

- Some large employers set up their own 501c3 tax-exempt nonprofit entities to enable employees to receive financial gifts tax-free.

TEACH FINANCIAL LITERACY.

It may be wise to require your team members to participate in a company-sponsored and company-facilitated financial literacy course to be eligible to get a need funded by the employee giving fund. Dave Ramsey's *Financial Peace University* would be an ideal program to offer to your team members.

Yes, pay good wages and teach financial literacy to your team members. But also ensure you have a system in place to ensure your team members aren't suffering in silence with financial burdens they can't carry alone.

REFLECTION, DISCUSSION, AND APPLICATION

Do you view your team members as part of your "household?"

What sustainable system will you implement (or have you already implemented) to help financially support employees facing occasional financial burdens they are unable to carry with their wages alone?

---

[1] C12 Business Forums (with Demos Restaurants), "Giving in the Name of Jesus," YouTube, October 27, 2021, educational video, https://www.youtube.com/watch?v=A7bwySSTLTU&t=84s

HELP THOSE WHO ARE AT-RISK AND/OR NEED A FIRST OR SECOND CHANCE

Our company operates a vocational training program for those who are at-risk and/or need first-chance or second-chance job experience and mentorship.

Now when you reap the harvest of your land, you shall not reap to the very edges of your field, nor shall you gather the gleanings of your harvest. And you shall not glean your vineyard, nor shall you gather the fallen grapes of your vineyard; you shall leave them for the needy and for the stranger. I am the Lord your God.

—Leviticus 19:9-10

One who is gracious to a poor person lends to the Lord, and He will repay him for his good deed.

—Proverbs 19:17

ncient Israel established laws regarding the harvesting of crops, which ensured that the "alien, the orphan, and the widow" were allowed to reap the gleanings of the fields (see Deut. 24:19-22; Lev. 19:9-10; 23:22; cf. Exod. 23:10-11; Ruth 2:1-10). The gleanings were the corners of the fields to be left for the needy to harvest for themselves. Although the gleanings were the overflow of the harvest, they were not free handouts that would require no work on the part of the beneficiary. Physical labor would be necessary to harvest those areas left for them.

What are the *gleanings* of your company? In other words, what are some tasks and responsibilities in your business that could be entrusted to people who either need a first chance (i.e., teenagers, single mothers, etc.) or a second chance (i.e., ex-convicts) to gain job experience in a Christ-centered environment?

PROVIDE FIRST-CHANCE JOB OPPORTUNITIES AND MENTORSHIP.

I have often lamented that my first few job experiences as a teenager (e.g., working at restaurants) resulted in an extremely poor introduction to the marketplace from a Christian discipleship standpoint. As far as I knew, there were no Christians working at my places of employment, and I certainly wasn't one either. My co-workers were older than me, and most of them didn't seem to have any sense of positive direction for their lives, so they were in no position to make a positive impact on me.

As with most teenagers I've known, my first experiences in the marketplace were vastly different from the Hebrew model in which a boy's first work experience was in his father's business. For example, Jesus worked in Joseph's carpentry business, and James and John worked in their father Zebedee's fishing business.

But our society has changed radically from the best practices of 1st-century Israel. Today, most people work jobs at companies they do not own where it is not feasible to take their kids to work for meaningful job experience and Christian workplace discipleship.

However, there are still at least two million companies worldwide — with at least $1 million in revenue and at least five employees — owned by Christian men and women who can provide a Christ-centered introduction to the workplace the next generation desperately needs.

Dave Hataj, second-generation owner of Edgerton Gear (Wisconsin), has been teaching and facilitating a course for high school students called *Craftsmen with Character*, which includes on-the-job experience at the Edgerton Gear factory. Dave understands most of these young people will neither stay in Edgerton nor work at his factory after they graduate from high school. Nevertheless, he's willing to invest in these young people and help reveal Father God's heart for them by taking them under his wing and giving them some valuable mentorship and work experience.

Provide Job Opportunities and Mentorship to People Who Are At-Risk and/or Need a Second Chance.

Hasson Painting ensures at least 5 percent of its workforce consists of at-risk employees (e.g., single mothers who don't have job training, ex-convicts, former drug addicts, people coming out of rehab, etc.). Company owner and CEO Bob Hasson said,

> 50 percent transition well. 50 percent don't. Although it's a major struggle for everyone involved, it's totally worth it for these people and for the Kingdom!

Barnhart Crane and Rigging operates a ministry for ex-convicts called Economic Opportunities, which provides job opportunities and mentorship for people released from incarceration. Some of these people gain employment at Barnhart, but the program helps most of them get hired elsewhere. Alan Barnhart told me,

> Approximately 7000 people come out of prison in our county each year. What these people need is Jesus and a job. They don't need a chance. They need intensive care. They need somebody looking after them to help them become employable, advocates we call "shepherds."

Consider partnering with a local prison ministry in your area and finding out how your company may be able to help soften the landing for men and women coming out of prison.

START AN INTERN PROGRAM.

Starting an intern program may be an ideal way for your company to provide job experience and mentorship for those who need it most. Yes, invite the best and brightest to apply for your internship program. But also give opportunities to those who need a first-chance or second-chance job. Graciously giving a job opportunity and mentorship to someone who seems to have little to offer your company can be a means of "lend[ing] to the Lord," and God promises "He will repay" (Prov. 19:17). Always remember that our primary purpose in business is not just to make a profit but to "make disciples" (Matt. 28:18).

REFLECTION, DISCUSSION, AND APPLICATION

What first-chance job opportunities and mentorship can your company provide?

What second-chance job opportunities and mentorship can your company provide?

CONCLUSION

THE FLOW OF SHALOM

Trust in the Lord with all your heart, and do not lean on your own understanding. In all your ways acknowledge Him, and He will make your paths straight.

—Proverbs 3:5-6

lite athletes aim to operate in a state of peak performance known as *flow* in which their bodies, instincts, preparation, and positive attitude are working together at optimal levels. In a state of flow, these athletes achieve the optimal swing, stride, throw, or shot as every part is gracefully working together.

In addition to paying the price for our sins, Jesus was tortured and crucified so we would experience the *flow* of total well-being, both individually and corporately. The Bible says, "The punishment for our *peace* was upon Him" (Isa. 53:5, emphasis mine). In this verse, the Hebrew word for "peace" is *shalom*, which means "well-being, totality, comprehensiveness, wholeness, nothing missing, nothing broken." God wants us to be faithful managers of everything he entrusts to us, for he has called us to "be holy in *all* respects" (1 Pet. 1:15), to "please Him in *all* respects" (Col. 1:10), to "grow up in *all* aspects" (Eph. 4:15), and ultimately, to "prosper in *all* respects" (3 John 2). By partnering with the Holy Spirit and obeying God's Word, we will experience the *flow of shalom*, embracing his best for our lives and for the companies we influence.

What would the *flow of shalom* look like for your company as a whole? If you were truly to "acknowledge Him in *all* your ways" (Prov. 3:6), seeking to discover and apply his will in every aspect of your company, how might your company's habits, culture, and impact look different?

In this book, you've been encouraged to help your company grow into a mature, Christ-centered company by adopting 37 Bible-based business habits across your company's culture and operations. You and your team do not have to do it all yourself. In fact, you *cannot* do anything of what God is asking you to do in and through your company according to your own strength and that of your team members. With an "if-it's-to-be-it's-up-to-me" approach, we might be able to earn a profit and feel like we're socially responsible people, but none of that will matter to God if our flesh is the driving force behind it. If our companies are to fulfill their God-given purposes to be Christ-centered, the Christian believers in our companies must embrace the reality that, apart from the Holy Spirit of Jesus Christ, we can do "nothing" that will truly matter in eternity or even here and now (John 15:5).

As John the Baptist said, "He must increase; I must decrease" (John 3:30). Yes, we must decrease. At the same time, allow God's limitless power and perfect wisdom to arise in you and your company, becoming its driving and guiding force through the Person of the Holy Spirit. The Holy Spirit wants to make you and your company's culture and business habits Christ-centered, and he is with you always to perform this supernatural work of grace.

ACKNOWLEDGEMENTS

A s iron sharpens iron, many people have contributed to the development and publishing of this book.

Thank you to my wonderfully wise wife, Marie, for helping me talk through the concepts in this book as I've been developing them over the past 10 years. As always, your encouragement, insights, and feedback make me so much better than I would be without you. Thank you for establishing a Christ-centered culture in our home and modeling the character of Jesus for me and our boys every day.

Thank you to Sarah Berry, Kimberly Lippencott, and the team at High Bridge Books & Media for helping to cultivate a Christ-centered culture and helping us apply these "habits" within our company.

Thank you to Rick Griest at Rosedale Bible College for being the earliest adopter of this curriculum and a key partner in its development.

Thank you to Dr. Ernest Liang and the Center for Christianity in Business at Houston Christian University for supporting this project with your wealth of wisdom.

Thank you to the members of Cornerstone Advisory Groups, especially Walt Taylor, for helping me to refine the content of this book and the assessment that goes along with it.

Finally, thank you to the many Christ-centered company influencers referenced in this book for modeling what it looks like to allow Jesus to be the center of your companies. You are my heroes.

Follow this QR code to take the
Christ-Centered Company Assessment.

THE CHRIST-CENTERED
COMPANY
WORKSHOP & GROUPS

If you would like Darren Shearer to facilitate a Christ-Centered Company Workshop in your local area and/or if you would like to join a Christ-Centered Company Virtual Group, please contact Darren via Darren@HighBridgeBooks.com.

Other books by Darren Shearer

The Marketplace Christian:
A Practical Guide to Using Your Spiritual Gifts in Business

Marketing Like Jesus:
25 Strategies to Change the World

In You God Trusts:
The Five Domains of Personal Responsibility

The Little Kids' Bible:
The Amazing Story of God's Rescue Plan for the World
(co-authored with Marie Shearer)

ABOUT THE AUTHOR

Darren Shearer is the founder and director of the Theology of Business Institute, which helps marketplace Christians explore and apply God's will for business. He has authored five books, including *Marketing Like Jesus: 25 Strategies to Change the World* and *The Marketplace Christian: A Practical Guide to Using Your Spiritual Gifts in Business*.

Darren is also the founder and CEO of High Bridge Books & Media, a multimedia agency specializing in publishing and promoting the world-changing ideas of Christ-centered influencers. Its imprint has published more than 175 books since 2013.

A former Captain in the United States Air Force, Darren earned the United States Air Force Commendation Medal for his meritorious service in Kuwait during Operation Iraqi Freedom.

He holds a M.A. in Practical Theology from Regent University (Virginia Beach, VA), an Advanced Graduate Certificate in Management from Pace University (New York, NY), and a B.A. in English from Charleston Southern University (Charleston, SC).

Darren and his wife, Marie, reside in the Great Smoky Mountains of Western North Carolina with their three young boys.

To connect with Darren or to contact him about speaking at an upcoming event, you may contact him via the following:

- E-mail: Darren@ HighBridgeBooks.com
- Web: www.TheologyofBusiness.com/contact
- LinkedIn: www.linkedin.com/in/darren-shearer-44232635
- Twitter: @DarrenShearer
- Facebook: www.Facebook.com/BusinessTheology

Made in the USA
Middletown, DE
21 May 2023

30663238R00161